WHO AUTHORIZED YOU TO QUIT?

Church Growth in "At-Risk" Communities

A New Developmental
Strategy
to Elevate People

ROGER BAKER

WHO AUTHORIZED YOU TO QUIT?:
CHURCH GROWTH IN "AT-RISK" COMMUNITIES

This book is written to provide information and motivation to readers. Its purpose is not to render any type of psychological, legal, or professional advice of any kind. The content is the sole opinion and expression of the author, and not necessarily that of the publisher.

Printed in the United States of America.

ISBN   978-1-64552-074-0   (Hardback)
ISBN   978-1-949746-89-1   (Paperback)
ISBN   978-1-949746-90-7   (Digital)

Lettra Press books may be ordered through booksellers or by contacting:

Lettra Press LLC
18229 E 52nd Ave.
Denver City, CO 80249
1 303 586 1431 | info@lettrapress.com
www.lettrapress.com

CONTENTS

SECTION 1

THE THEOLOGICAL TASK
(CALL TO EXODUS)

STATEMENT OF APOLOGY

The person who begins behind in the race must run faster than the person ahead to catch up and win. This suggests two questions:

1. How far ahead is the lead runner?
2. How far is it to the finish line?

The African American did not start the race at the starting line alongside European Americans. If we use 1619 as the starting point (the year when African Americans first arrived in Jamestown), the Negro did not even enter the race until 346 years later, with the Voting Rights Act of 1965. African Americans, you have been running for only forty-eight years, and you are not *authorized to quit!*

The historical background of the black women must be shared for us to get a better understanding of the underlying psychological effects suffered by many single-parent females today. That background information may come across to many— the Eurocentric, black elitists who have forgotten they are still Negroes, and many immigrants who may read through these pages—as a militant attack upon them. This is neither the intent nor the purpose of the information.

This information is also for those who feel black people started out in America at the same starting point as others and that they faced the same obstacles and benefitted from the same opportunities as others. Many such people are ignorant of the reason black people are in the deficit they find themselves in. Real black history is forbidden in public schools, and rightly so. It is too gruesome to discuss in a classroom without causing riots and killings in the school.

In the following pages, I lean very heavily on the black church. The black church is the only strategic institution African Americans are cable of claiming in their neighborhood. Sadly, it seems that they have become too heavenly bound to be any earthly good. There is a saying: the same thing it took to get it is not sufficient in increasing its value; it requires more. The black church must get back into the business of developing character, leadership, and entrepreneurial principles in poor people. The time is right to pressure the government and others for financial resources to assist the black churches because the churches are properly equipped for holistic family development. Gang activities and crime of all sorts—which come out of the poverty-stricken at-risk African-American communities—are affecting this nation severely. In reality, our choices are "pay less now" or "pay much more lately."

The information in this book is based on the premise that everything from eternity past through eternity future is on God's divine timeline of history and exists for His purpose. Through faith alone, in Christ alone does God exist, reveal Himself, make sense, and work out His plan for creation. Since humanity is the object of God's plan, humanity owes God a hearing. In light of that firm belief, I will continue to work on my PhD in personal and human development in the University of Reality, where

- God the Father is the author;
- God the Son, the Lord Jesus Christ, is the Creator of all things and the dean of all affairs; and
- God the Holy Spirit is the Counselor, motivator, Sustainer,
- Comforter, revealer, and teacher.

Also, I solicit your Trinitarian—God the Father, God the Son, and God the Holy Spirit—prayers for a deeper revelation of holistic at-risk family development. The information that follow is true and can lead to profound approaches in reducing at-risk crimes and in developing 80 percent of the socioeconomically disadvantaged within fifteen to twenty years of its implementation.

A SPECIAL MESSAGE TO THE READER

As Paul waited in the city of Athens, he became upset by seeing all the idols the people worshiped. However, he noticed an altar with the words, "To the Unknown God" (Acts 17:23c). The Council (the Areopagus) brought Paul before them and said, "Tell us what your new teaching is about. We have heard you say some strange things, and we want to know what you mean" (Acts 19:20).

The principles of yesterday in the Holy Bible still apply today. I find in America many religious altars hidden under the banner of Christianity. Therefore, it is essential that, for the purpose of this publication, readers understand that the Holy Bible is God Himself speaking to us.

God is always divinely guiding those who have faith alone in the Lord Jesus Christ alone. When the ominous clouds of uncertainty obscure our path, the radiant light of God's Word pierces the darkness to illuminate our way. Our God is like this forever and will always guide us (Psalm 48:14).

In Hebrews 4:12—13, the author writes:

> What God has said isn't only alive and active! It is sharper than any double-edged sword. His word can cut through our spirits and souls and through our joints and marrow, until it covers the desires and thoughts of our hearts.
>
> Everything in the Scriptures is God's Word. All of it is useful for teaching and helping people and for correcting them and showing them how to live. The Scriptures train God's servants to do all kinds of good deeds. (2 Timothy 3:16-17)

Every Christian at salvation becomes both priest and ambassador, and as priest and ambassadors, we must do our best to win God's approval as workers who don't need to be ashamed and who teach only the true message of God (2 Timothy 2:15).

> As an ambassador, Paul taught the athenians the true message of the "Unknown God."
> This God made the world and everything in it. He is Lord of the heaven and earth and He doesn't live in temples built by human hands. He doesn't need help from anyone. He gives life, breath, and everything else ... (Acts 17:24ff)
> There is only one God, and Christ Jesus is the only one who can bring us to God. Jesus was truly human, and He gave Himself to rescue all of us. (1 Timothy 2:5)

The Six Building Blocks for Success

This document is written from the author's understanding of the six building blocks of success that are the core to understanding life:

- Scripture
- Tradition
- Experience
- Reason
- Practice
- Faith

"Faith that doesn't lead us to do good deeds is all alone and dead" (James 2:17). Learning without doing is like not learning at all. The best way to get people to learn something is to turn them into teachers. It is only in the doing and applying that knowledge and understanding are internalized (The Eighth Habit, 32). "All children are born geniuses; 9,999 out of every 10,000 are swiftly, inadvertently degeniusized by grownups" (Buckminster Fuller).

Tradition has not favored African Americans in establishing a vision, a mission, objectives, and goals. Under the white-supremacy paternalist caste system, these privileges have been denied through social and economic conditions. Even today all African Americans are at-risk. Everything we have can be taken away by the US government without legitimate reason and can become irretrievable. No organizations, whether schools, colleges, universities, seminaries, or religious orders, are designed to address the pariah. Pariah is defined as one who is despised or rejected (i.e., outcast).

The federal and state governments have failed in their attempt to meet the pariah's need for holistic development. Public and private schools are inept. Either out of ignorance or stupidity, colleges, universities, and seminaries fail to prepare their students to educate and develop the black population, which is 14 percent of the total population—42 million of America's total 350 million. Ignorance is when you don't know; stupid is when you know yet refuse to do.

There has been enough grant money to lift up the backwash that got caught in the civil rights movement and the War on Drugs. It has been the passionate endeavor of philanthropists or donors to deliver those struggling to open the doors in African-American communities for further exploiting. The money chasers—expert grant writers—found an opportunity to increase their standard of living by courting the money donors for at-risk people. Their mission and vision is written with an eagle's eye view, looking only from the outside rather than from a worm's-eye view. A worm sees the nutrient that enters the root that makes the fruit. An eagle is a high flier and sees only the fruit. It tries to judge the fruit by its cover.

To the organizations that are designed to educate and develop the at-risk, if travel education is not in the holistic education and development initiative at least once a week, that program is a failure. You cannot educate holistically when you are confined to the ghetto. Therefore, travel education must consist of exposure and practice with a focus on character, leadership, and entrepreneurial principles. Social development requires inventing new ways to bring about a vision of life, and that requires travel. Therefore, it is best to leave the grant money with the grantor.

The pariah African American does not become a citizen of America. Citizenship is one America, not white Americans and black Americans. Since we are two Americas, the black church is the only hope. All African-American at-risk communities are redlined by banks—property too risky to invest in. Therefore, the community churches must focus on preparing, inspiring, and empowering tomorrows business leaders. This requires a twenty-first-century holistic family-development institution.

In the twenty-first century, the business of America is education. Nothing is more vital to the competitiveness and advancement of corporations, both large and small, than a literate, tech-capable, and critical-thinking workforce. Available jobs unfulfilled represent money that is not circulating in the economy. To prepare a productive individual, the attempt must begin before conception. In many national regions there is a continuous demand for qualified skilled individuals. And Step, Incorporated's "Train-Up a Child" nurturing/ mentoring model is designed for success and for benefiting self, the family, the nation, and the world.

Original "And Step" Document

The original And Step document was written between January 1995 and June 1995. A copy was shared with Baker's bishop, George W. Bashore, resident bishop of the Western Pennsylvania United Methodist Conference. On August 11, 1995, he wrote:

> Dear Roger,
> Recently I completed reading your paper, "Strategy to Elevate People." I want to thank you for sharing a copy with me. Your insights, gathering of pertinent information and challenges are most helpful, and I hope you will be able to use rhe paper as a base for dialogue and motivation. I pray that your new responsibilities will go well and that you will discover Christ at the center of all you do. Grace, peace, and joy! (See exhibit 1—George W. Bashore.)
>
> George

And Seep was born in Ambridge, Pennsylvania, in an effort to start a new African-American congregation in Ambridge, a borough that was for the European upper middle class during the steel days. In those days, the Negro could live only in Aliquippa, a segregated section a mile away from Ambridge called Plan 11. Between 1920 and 1970, the Jones & Laughlin Steel Company attracted many immigrant workers from southern and eastern Europe and blacks from the impoverished Southern states. The process of assimilation of the Negro into this part of the country was marked by a large degree of turmoil, hate, violence, and bigotry, all of which continue to this present day.

In 1991, the Western Pennsylvania United Methodist Annual Conference recruited Rev. Roger W. Baker from the North Texas United Methodist Annual Conference to start a Black United Methodist Church (Fellowship) at 550 Maplewood Avenue in Ambridge, Pennsylvania. At 649 Maplewood Avenue in Ambridge, Pennsylvania, the First United Methodist Church stood in operation. Baker arrived in Ambridge, Pennsylvania, on November 1,1991, and departed briefly in January 1995 with the core leadership in place. While at the Pittsburgh Theological Seminary on sabbatical leave from January 1995 to June 30, 1995, Baker wrote the original "And Step." Today, Fellowship is operating under the name Center for Hope at 740 Park Road (www.centerforhope.com). One must keep in mind that starting Fellowship was not without strong opposition, even to the point that the pastor of the First United Methodist Church's family was threatened, and his car was badly damaged and much more. The United Methodist Conference had to transfer him to save his life.

In the *Beaver County Times,* Lotya Ann Eaglrston wrote in 1993 under the heading "Social Ministry: Methodist ministry establishes church in Ambridge that attracts children and adults who are poor and at-risk":

> He uses overhead projectors and a third-grade version of the Bible during Sunday sermons. Most of his congregation members are children, and bowling,

skating and grocery shopping is as much a part of his ministry as preaching.

The Rev. Roger Baker is reaching "the very people the Bible tells us we ought to be reaching, and we don't do it very often," said Erwin Kerr, district superintendent of the three-county Butler District of the United Methodist Church.

Brought to Ambridge in 1991 to open church that would serve the growing black population, Baker found it difficult to set up a traditional church in the urban setting. He also found people hurting and in need.

More than a year into the job, Baker's work Fellowship United Methodist Church has become social ministry that attracts children and adults who are poor and at-risk. And Baker has attracted the attention of national official in the United Methodist Church, who is considering the church as a model for Urban-Ministry. "I would say we are at a turning point," Kerr said. He plans to meet with clergy from local churches today to set up an advisory group for the church.

Baker's church, which opened in the spring in 1992, has about 65 regular members — 20 of whom are adults, Baker said. Most of these people come from troubled backgrounds that involved drugs, unemployment and welfare. Baker, 49, tries to reach them on a basic level, making the church an administration site for Women, Infants and Children program that provides food vouchers for new mothers and their children. He also spends Saturdays taking the children on bowling, skating or YMCA outings.

"We put a lot of emphasis on respecting self and other people's property. We put them in a setting, watch how they act and coach them along in that," said Baker, who moved to Ambridge from Dallas. He also hopes to start a parenting and nurturing program for adults In January, as well as a career mentoring program for the young people.

Louis Hill left his church in Aliquippa for Fellowship because "this ministry right here is for who seem to be shutout by other churches that are supposedly so Christian-minded." "He spends a lot of time with the few members he's got," said Hill, 46. of Aliquippa, "He takes those shopping, takes their babies to the doctor; take the women to the Laundromat. This way, he's got the opportunity to minister to the members one by one."

Fellowship is just the kind of ministry that the declining United Methodist Church needs, said Clyde Anderson, executive secretary for the office of New Church Development at the General Board of Global Ministries for the Methodist Church. In the past 10 years, church membership has declined from about 11 million to 8 million. "I think we're losing because there is a lack of vision for what the church is to be," Anderson said.

Kerr said, "I don't think we're typically inclusive in our local churches." The reason?

"Racism." If the interracial church becomes a ministry model, the national church could provide limited financial help as well as training in leadership and fundraising.

Ultimately, Baker envisions a regional church that would serve all of Beaver County. "As I look at the cities across the nation and how communities are drug-infested and children are in danger and churches are not reaching out to them," he said, "I think the nation needs ministers called to do that type of ministry."

For Bonita Thompson, 29, of Ambridge, the church "feels like a family, like we're part of it." "I've come from a pretty bad situation in my life," said the single mother of two. "I needed a church. A lot of things went on in my life that I sought God. My life is better now." And after only a few months at the church, she already serves on church committees.

"It's really teaching me about how a church runs by being on church committees, whereas before you have to be in a church 50 years" to get on a committee, she said. "At some of the older churches everybody is set in their ways. You know how older people are."

INTRODUCTION

Jesus plumbed, the uttermost depths of the human situation so there would be no places we might go where He has not been before. The strategy to elevate people is for everyone. No human being knows everything. We learn from each other, and even in the church we learn and practice on each other. Everyone should remember that this earthly life is just a rehearsal of the life to come. If we are practicing evil (religion) then our eternal fate is the "lake of fire and burning sulphur," hell eternal with Satan and his demons (Revelation 20:7-15). If we are practicing Christianity, our destiny is with the Lord Jesus Christ in the "New Heaven and the New Earth" (Revelation 21fiF). The angelic conflict between Satan and God is over at the judgment.

To elevate people, we must discover where they are socially, economically, psychologically, physically, and spiritually. Once we make that assessment, by the guidance of the Holy Spirit, we become able to elevate them to the next level one step at a time by "nurturing and mentoring" them. Our task as Christians is to nurture and mentor and let God do the elevating. If we go forth in faith, we shall be victorious in Jesus Christ. "He or she that goes forth weeping, bearing the seed for sowing, shall come home with shouts of joy, bringing his or her sheaves with them." (Psalm 126:6)

To understand people, we must first listen for a complete understanding before being understood. Many times what we learn first is something about ourselves. What we learn about ourselves may or may not please us. Those who are above the poverty line (middle class and upper middle class) observe what life is about from the perspective of the poor who must go without. The poor (border line poverty and below) can observe what life is about from the perspective of the wealthy in reference to the material abundance of life.

The poor most likely will never obtain riches, but observing others who have obtained riches gives them a sense of hope, and for some it gives them joy. We must keep in mind that being poor does not advocate immorality. As a matter of fact, I believe some of those who are poor are more virtuous than some of those who are wealthy. When the Virgin Mary gave birth to Jesus, she dressed Him in baby clothes and laid Him on a bed of hay because there was no room for them in the inn (Luke 2:7). The Baby was God Almighty, the Creator of all things, seen and unseen, both in the heavens and on the earth (Colossians 1:17).

And Step, Inc.'s "Train-Up a Child" nurturing/mentoring model is about elevating the poor, specifically the poor black children and youth who deserve a chance to explore life. To help the poor black children, we must try to elevate their parents or guardians. In this book I target the black single female parent, who is locked into the public welfare system. This system is their lifeline, and very few escape.

Many of them have dreams and goals, and for some reason, they are not being pursued. However, there are some who are pursuing their dreams and goals, even though it is very complicated. For the moment, I will focus on those who are complacent and those who are not pursuing their dreams and goals. Most likely these are people who have not been motivated to dream and plan for the future. The danger in this complacency is that they are not exploring their talents and gifts, which could lead them to riches.

They may not have experienced love during their early childhood and adolescent years (between childhood and adulthood, ages eleven to eighteen). Maybe they are orphans, and child/youth services placed them with several foster parents. As a child, their parents may have experienced rejection by family members, peers, teachers, preachers, the community, and even their own local church congregations. Abuse breathes abuse. If the child is abused, it cause a major setback in his or her ability to learn. The fear of abuse contributes to low self-esteem and low self-concept.

For the female, the above may have played an important part in early pregnancies. Many are not educated in controlling their sexual passion in the moment of weakness. It is not uncommon for ten- or eleven-year-olds to become pregnant. Fear, anger, resentment, hatred, jealousy, and guilt prevent them from peace of mind, and life becomes very difficult. If they do not have enough problems by being young mothers, the Christian community sometimes puts the icing on the cake by condemning and spiritually abandoning them. One of the things the Christian community needs to improve in is forgiveness and unconditional love. Even when teenagers and adults have abortions, we should respect them and pray God's glory on them. The Virgin Mary was thirteen when she gave birth to our Lord and Savior Jesus the Christ.

In Jawanza Kunjufu' book *Hip-Hop vs. MAAT,* he uses the terms *pro-life* and *pro-death.* I have to agree with his statement when he referred to the Republican Party and the Conservative Democrats. Jawanza says, "There is a contradiction for politicians to advocate life and then not properly fund Head-Start, Chapter 1 Pell Grants, and employment opportunities while allocating 1/3 of the Federal budget to the military" (137).

If Christians support resolutions against abortion, why not make and support resolutions to expose poor black and white children to higher educational values? This will require free travel outside of their community. There should be funding for all at-risk children and youth who attend a summer sports camp and travel out of state for at least a three to seven-day education study each year. Study has sho wn that at-risk children and youth forget 40 to 60 percent of classroom material during summer break, yet they only learned 55 percent of the subject during the school year

And Step, Inc.

And Step, Inc., is about empowering the weak by removing the veil so they may see the love of God and approach God's presence through Jesus Christ as it is revealed by the Holy Spirit. For this to happen, the faith community must abandon its prejudice, its false dignity, and its pride and humbly pick up its cross and follow Christ. "Be united in what you think, as if you were only one person. Don't be jealous or proud, but be humble and consider others more important than yourselves. Care about them as much as you care about yourselves" (Philippians 2:2b—4). Those who deny themselves and follow Christ do so because they know the following:

1. The tomb has lost its power.
2. The grave has lost its terror.
3. Death has lost its tragedy.

THE AUTHOR

Once a person puts his or her hands to the plow, there is no turning back unless he or she wants to go back. The author had a limited early education (grades one through twelve) as a sharecropper (one step above slavery) and attending a segregated school when it rained and after harvest. He was born December 7, 1943, in Gatesville, North Carolina. This restricts his writing and communication ability among the European elite and African American eloquently cultured. He was born to a sharecropper (one step above slavery) who attended school until the fourth grade and a mother who attended until the ninth. To both the elitist and eloquently cultured, he is seen as a pariah (the lowest of the social caste) and as at-risk. His nickname is Just Barely:

- He just barely graduated from a segregated school in 1962 using textbooks three editions older than white county schools.
- He just barely made it into the US Army and retired as a combat army drill sergeant after twenty-two years of service. By federal designation, once one is a drill sergeant (which the author became in 1967 upon returning from Vietnam), it is eternal.
- He just barely earned his Texas life and health insurance license in 1975.
- He just barely received his Texas real estate license in 1976 and his Texas real estate broker's license in 1980.
- He just barely received his Texas investment broker's license in 1984.

- He just barely earned his bachelor's degree in business administration (finance and economics) in 1984.
- He just barely earned a four-year master of divinity degree in three years in 1987 from Southern Methodist University (SMU).
- He was just barely ordained as an eider by the United Methodist North Texas Annual Conference in 1990.
- In 1999, he just barely received his Pennsylvania state life and health license.
- He just barely received his Pennsylvania investment broker's license in 2002.
- He was proficient in Pastoring ten churches as the change agent over a fifteen-year period, and two of the churches were European white, with over thirty millionaires in each.
- Presently he is a congregation and community development specialist, and the world is his parish.
- As a quadripareses (incomplete quadriplegic), he moves only with a walker. This is military connected without military compensation.
- He is motivated by God the Holy Spirit to educate America.

It is his vernacular (lack of diphthong and phonetics use) and his Southern accent that marks him as dumb or ignorant. Even though he is considered to be dumb or ignorant, his assertive voice is for the development of mind, body, and spirit of the socioeconomically disadvantaged and at- risk. Every soul must stand before the Lord Jesus (Philippians 2:10). The human soul is the rational, immaterial aspect of humankind, composed of self-consciousness/awareness, mentality, volition, and consciousness *(lhe Plan ofGody* 2).

The Lord's message to the author is the same as Ezekiel's to the nation of Israel:

> [Roger W. Baker], I am sending you to your own people ... All of them are stubborn and hardheaded, so I will make you as stubborn as they are. You will be so determined to speak My message that nothing will stop

you. I will make you hard like a diamond, and you will
have no reason to be afraid of those arrogant rebels.
(Ezekiel 3:4—9)

A Call to Liberation Theology

The Spirit of the Lord is in me. As a Christian soldier, I must continue
to march forward into the battle of government (federal and state)
inept considerations of the socioeconomically disadvantaged and
at- risk. The apostle Paul in Ephesians 6:11 tell us, "Put on all the
armor that God gives, so you can defend yourselves against the
devil's tricks." Why do we need armor if there is no war? The
battle is against ignorance (lack of knowledge), prejudice (judging
without facts), false pride, false dignity, greed, and treachery. All
of us are ignorant to a degree, and for this reason, it is relevant for
each of us to keep a filling of God the Holy Spirit. The filling of the
Holy Spirit is required of Christians. Christianity is not a religion
but a relationship with Jesus Christ by grace through faith alone.

Religion is an anti-grace system whereby an individual by his
or her good works, effort, and merit seeks to gain salvation or the
approbation of God. Religion is Satan's ace trump to counterfeit
Christianity by diverting the believer through moral or immoral
degeneracy from executing God's plan, will, and purpose for his
or her life. The satanic religious system of thinking, values, or
problem solving encourages human arrogance and sponsors human
antagonism to God (Mental Attitude Dynamics, 4-5). It was and is the
Devil's system of religion that wreaks havoc and upheaval to the
African slaves in America. God created every human mind with
freedom of thought and freedom of choice, and He holds everyone
responsible for what he or she thinks or chooses.

Black liberation theology is a humanistic mind-set that attempts
to focus Christian theology on the plight of the poor being liberated
from all forms of bondage and injustice, whether real or perceived,
whether social, political, economic, or religious. Its primary goal
is to make Christianity real to blacks living in at-risk African-
American communities.

Christ came to earth to unite all who believe in Him in one universal church, His body, of which He is the head (Ephesians 1:22—23). Members of the body of Christ share a common bond with all other Christians, regardless of background, race, or nationality. "There should be no division in the body, but... its parts should have equal concern for each other" (1 Corinthians 12:25). As such, we are to be of one mind, having the mind of Christ and having the goal of glorifying God by fulfilling Christ's command to "go into all the world," telling others about Him, preaching the good news of the gospel, and teaching others to observe His commandments (Matthew 28:19-20). Jesus reminds us that the two greatest commandments are to love God and love others as ourselves.

SECTION 2

THE NEGRO DEFICIT
(TRADITIONAL RACIAL DISPARITY)

CONDITION OF BLACK
SINGLE WOMEN

Our mental attitudes determine, motivate, and influence our behavior and actions. The right lobe of the mentality of the soul relates to the thought pattern. The right lobe is full knowledge: the heart and mind. The left or perceptive lobe is the staging area for knowledge. After expressing faith alone in Christ alone, people acquire human spirits in which the Holy Spirit takes their academic knowledge (left lobe) and transfers it by faith into full knowledge (right lobe) as they focus on divine viewpoints through Bible doctrine. "Divine viewpoint is the thinking value system, and problem-solving ability gleaned from Bible doctrine, an orientation of life based on God's perspective" *(Mental Attitude Dynamics^ 2)*. When doctrine norms and standards are created in the conscience, one grows and develops spiritually and experiences the divine viewpoint. There is a connection between physical health and thought patterns. Continuous mental tension, such as fear, worry, and anxiety, will eventually overflow and affect the body. With an overflow of pressures from the mind to the body, people may suffer from eczema, skin rashes, warts, allergies, asthma, hypertension, goiter, ulcers, and many other disorders. Jesus died on the cross for sin so everyone may experience inner peace and have a relaxed mental attitude, stability, and inner happiness. However, Satan, through his orderly, cohesive, and multifaceted system of imperialism attacked the mind through slavery.

Slavery (www. Willie lynch letter: the making of a slave.com)
WWW.the final call-willie lynch letter: the making of a slave.com

Willie Lynch, a slave owner in the West Indies, made a speech in 1712 on the James River's banks in the colony of Virginia. He shared a method of slave control. His method included continuous indoctrination of fear, distrust, and envy. Included in the indoctrination was also the separation of the young males and females and the old males and females. Also, they were to be separated by color (light vs. dark). "The goal was to get the slaves to only trust, depend, love, and respect white servants and overseers, the plantation masters.

Since the arrival of the first twenty human beings from Africa in 1619 to Jamestown, Virginia, to work in the tobacco fields, black Americans have been isolated, alienated, depressed, and hopeless.

The West Africa people were seized from tribes in the interior of the continent by European and Arab slave traders and rival tribes; then they were sold to America by the Dutch, Portuguese, the Spanish, and the English sea dog John Hawkins. Even though the population of slaves was low in the 1600s, the colonial government took drastic steps to institutionalize slavery.

In 1662 Virginia passed a law that automatically made slaves of slaves' children. Maryland's assembly in 1664 declared that all Negroes in the colony were slaves for life. And New York's legislators recognized in 1684 that slavery was a legitimate practice. From 1670 to 1708, Virginia's slave population grew from two thousand to twelve thousand. Slaves in the Southern colonies were agriculture workers, and in the Northern colonies, Africans were domestic servants *(US History for Dummies,* 46-47). Imperialism was at work to establish its policies and practices by extending its power and dominion in America.

When the US Constitution was written in 1787, the issue of slavery was avoided. The plantation system produced important cash crops for export, but it depended on the labor of the enslaved [Negroes]. One of the cash crops for export was cotton. In 1793, Eli Whitney invented the cotton gin, which removed cottonseeds quickly and cheap. Now cotton could be grown profitably anywhere in the South, which encouraged planters to acquire more land by moving westward. Through the 1850s, slaves produced most of the raw cotton for textile mills in Great Britain and in the northeastern part of the United States *(American Labor, Boy Scouts Merit Badge,* 7—10). Unlike the Africans being seized for slave labor, the Irish, German, Scandinavian, Chinese, and Italian immigrants entered America for labor opportunities. Industrial growth took off because opportunities for trade expanded. The Declaration of Independence inspired the immigrant workers to demand their rights as people created equal to business owners. Since the US Constitution declared slaves as only three-fifths of a human being, the slaves had no voice. A Mississippi Yazoo Delta planter in 1866 wrote:

> I think God intended the [Negroes] to be slaves. Now since man has deranged Gods plan, I think the best we can do is keep 'em as near to a state of bondage as possible ... my theory is "feed 'em well," "clothe 'em well," and then, if they don't work ... "whip 'em well." *(Worse than Slavery,* 11)

After Emancipation

After emancipation in 1865, millions of slaves, under the pressure of federal bayonets, were freed. The Mississippi State Legislature immediately went to work passing a series of acts known as the Black Codes. South Carolina, Georgia, Florida, Alabama, Louisiana, and Texas nearly copied the codes word for word and enforced them. These codes were vigorously enforced, and hundreds of the Negroes were arrested and auctioned off to local planters. Others scrubbed horses, swept sidewalks, and hauled away trash.

When the US Congress passed the 1867 Reconstruction Act, it was partly designed to encourage the South's four million ex-slaves to remain where they were. In Mississippi the act created a new political majority, with eighty thousand Negro voters over sixty thousand white voters. By 1870, Negroes were serving as sheriffs, mayors, state legislators, and speaker of the Mississippi House of Representative and the US Senate.

In 1870, the legislature passed Mississippi's first Public Education Law, guaranteeing four months of free schooling each year to all children regardless of race. Black hopes and white fears collided. Violence and vigilante action took on a distinctly racial air by the local rifle clubs like White Rose, Seventy-Six, and Sons of the South. The most notorious of them all was the Ku Klux Klan, known as the Invisible Empire *(Worse than Slavery, 26)*.

In Monroe County, a Klan mob made "Fried [Negro] meat" of a Republican leader by disemboweling him in front of his wife. By summer of 1871, not a Negro was in operation in the state of Mississippi *(Worse than Slavery, 21—27)*.

Convict leasing fully took hold in Mississippi in 1875. Jones S. Hamilton, a former county sheriff, state senator, and Confederate cavalry officer, was the primary lessee of the Mississippi state penitentiary in the late 1870s and 1880s. He became a millionaire by subleasing hundreds of convicts to railroad builders and plantation owners. In 1876, the legislature passed the Pig Law aimed directly at the Negro, which led to convict leasing. They were subleased at $1.75 a day. Chained for days in knee-deep pools of muck, drinking the water in which they were compelled to deposit their excrement, convicts dropped from exhaustion, pneumonia, malaria, frostbite, consumption, sunstroke, dysentery, gunshot wounds, and shackle poisoning. A planter wrote former George Washington Gable in 1883, "Before the war we owned the [Negro]. If a man had a good [Negro], he could afford to take care of him, if he was sick, get a doctor. He might even put gold plugs in his teeth. But these convicts we don't own them. One dies, get another!" *(Worse than Slavery, 55)*.

Pick a [Negro] to Lynch

June 1, 1921, was the day of the largest massacre of nonmilitary Americans in the history of this nation. The Ku Klux Klan destroyed "Black Wall Street" in Tulsa, Oklahoma. During this Negro holocaust, over three thousand men and women were killed and placed in mass graves all around the city. The area destroyed encompassed over six hundred businesses, thirty-six blocks, with a population of fifteen thousand Negroes. For the Ku Klux Klan, it was typical to have a picnic on a Friday evening in Oklahoma. The word is short for "pick a [negro]" to lynch. They would lynch a Negro male and cut off body parts as souvenirs every weekend (www.BlackWallStreet.com, 1—6).

African-American Females

The African-American female has been caught into a chain of events that have instilled hopelessness within her mind since the mid-sixteenth century. During slavery, she was exploited and sexually abused and had to give birth to a child once a year, with only two weeks to nurture her child. She was forced to have sex with men for whom she had no desire and was denied the privilege of raising her own children. Childbirth began at the beginning of puberty (when she was still a child). For many, they watched their own children being taken from them and sold to distant plantations. The black woman was forced to work the farmland like a nonstop machine. She was degraded to the lowest class of humanity and denied any time for self-education or to educate her offspring. These conditions occurred before and after World War I. Black women migrated to the North after World War I, with high hopes of a better life situation. If they were able to find work, it consisted of cooking, cleaning, washing, or other tedious, strenuous, and degrading occupations. After migrating to the North, she was responsible for transmitting the culture, customs, and values of the black community to her children. She was "The catalyst in the transition process from the rural South to the Urban North ... she was responsible for making a home in crowded and substandard housing, ... Many landlords refused housing to Black women with children" (Cannon, 61).

Even with these struggles, many black women were able to keep their families together. It has been the practice for many years for the white supremacy to break up the family unit by selling or trading children, youth, and adults to faraway plantations. There was very little family cohesion among slaves. The selling or trading of family members forced black women to be heads of their households. Even though family cohesiveness was allowed after slavery and after World War II, women continued to become heads of households. mainly because of marital instability, low remarriage continuation of out-of-wedlock birth. With no jobs, no income, and no family support in a highly industrial society, the single parent's only hope was the social welfare system (Cannon, 65).

The black woman has been affected by other conditions that also added to her hopelessness of ever being free of alienation, isolation, depression, and oppression, such as: the Korean and Vietnam Wars; the assassinations of John F. Kennedy, Robert Kennedy, and Martin Luther King Jr.; the Civil Rights Movement; the War on Drugs; and insensitive and inept federal government policymaking, which will further affect black families' livelihood. The death of Dr. Martin Luther King Jr. dates the dehumanizing practices on African Americans in this nation.

Ronald Reagans War on Drugs

Another date of dehumanizing practice on African Americans is in October of 1982, when President Ronald Reagan activated the African-American holocaust, the War on Drugs, a worse act than Adolf Hitler committed. The CIA admitted in 1998 that in the early 1980s, the guerilla armies they supported in Nicaragua were smuggling illegal drugs into the United States. These drugs made their way into the streets of inner-city black neighborhoods in the form of crack cocaine. They also admitted that, in the midst of the War on Drugs, they blocked law enforcement efforts to investigate illegal drug networks that were helping to fund its covert war in Nicaragua (Jhe New Jim Crow, 6)

The budget of the federal law enforcement agencies soared (ibid., 49):

- Between 1980 and 1984, FBI anti-drug funding increased from $33 million to $95 million.
- Department of Defense anti-drug allocations increased from $33 million in 1981 to $1,042 billion in 1991.

- During that same period, DEA anti-drug spending grew from $86 million to $181 million.
- FBI anti-drug allocations grew from $38 million to $181 million.

In 1985, the Reagan administration hired staff to publicize the emergence of crack cocaine as part of a strategic effort to build public and legislative support for the War on Drugs. The media was saturated with images of black "crack [prostitution]," "welfare queens," "crack dealers," and "crack babies." This media strategy was designed to create the worst negative racial stereotypes about impoverished inner-city African-American residents (ibid., p.5). The Reagan administration targeted black communities with crack cocaine over twenty-seven years ago (1983-85), costing America several trillion dollars and counting. This is what got him reelected. He went to Congress seventeen times, increasing the federal deficit to fund the War on Drugs. As a result, by targeting black men through the War on Drugs and decimating black communities, the US criminal justice system functions as a contemporary system of racial control by destroying the minds of poor African Americans to give the white middle class the competitive advantage.

A Reflection on the Nation

Education has not been privileged to many African Americans like the cultured Eurocentric Americans. Therefore, many black, single, poverty-stricken mothers should not be held accountable for what they don't know and are denied the privilege to learn. Therein lays a tremendous culture lag brought on by a capitalistic, unethical, morally corrupt, and vicious racist society. I say vicious racist society because many school systems are subtly designed by white supremacy to further humiliate black poor (pariah) children by ignoring their basic needs rather than practicing love.

It seems like the previous practices should cause this nation to be more sensitive to human hurt. Rather, it is getting progressively worse. The Federal Communication Commission allows radio programs and television shows to publicly denounce black people and degrade them to dogs or other animals and to be treated as objects. Even the federal, state, and county government police forces continue to advocate that black people are inferior. There seems to be an overtone that African Americans are causing this nation to experience social and economic hardship and are causing debt problem. Yet if it was not for the African slave, there be an American.

Let us reflect on a question. If this nation gave every African American who is unemployed and underemployed a free education up to a bachelor degree in five-years, would that minimize crime? Maybe it would, but maybe it would not. I believe white collar crime would rise and there would be fewer arrests. If this nation supported free education for the at-risk, there would not be a need for as many policemen, judges, jailers, wardens, prison guards, jail-building contractors, food stamps, social service workers, doctors, nurses, hospitals, etc. Rather, we would need more private housing, automobiles, bank loans, child care, adequate church education facilities, etc. Which race and class of people would benefit the most? Poor people always benefit the capitalists. This morally and ethically corrupt, capitalistic society does not hesitate to introduce ideology that conflicts with the biblical-grounded, God-given, moral principle-centered value system. Principles are universal, timeless, and self-evident. God is principle; He is the same yesterday, today, and forever. All people are created equal: "From one man God made every nation of people, that they should inhabit the whole earth; and He determined the times for them and the exact places where they should live" (Acts 17:26).

On the other hand, this nation's focus is on values. Values are social norms; they are personal, emotional, subjective, and arguable (*The Eight Habit*, 48-49) All people have values. The ratification of the US Constitution by the framing fathers, including President George Washington the slaveholder, says that African slaves are only three-fifths of a human being; this is value based. This is a violation of principle.

Therefore, predominately all African Americans are at-risk people. Traditionally black people identify with the Bible book of Exodus, which teaches the "Lord is the one true God and the ruler of all creation. And when the Lord decides to do something, no one can stop Him." That theology got lost after Dr. Martin Luther King Jr. death. Prosperity and Affirmative Action took center stage, creating a venerable pariah backwash. The Civil Rights Movement in the 1960s raised the issue of discrimination and challenged the unions' predominantly white male leadership. On April 4, 1968, Martin Luther King Jr. was assassinated in Memphis, Tennessee, where he had come to support a sanitation workers' strike.

National Facts about At-Risk African Americans

African Americans are 14 percent (42,020,743) of the US population.

- Sixty percent of all black males who drop out of high school spend time in prison before age thirty-five.
- Forty-four percent of the prison population is black.
- Thirty-three percent of the homeless are black men.
- Twenty-five percent of all black men are in prison, on probation, or on parole.
- Fifty percent of all black males drop out of high school.
- Young black male suicides increased 100 percent over the past decade.
- Ninety-four percent of all black people murdered are murdered by black people.
- Over eight thousand homicides a year are committed by black men.
- Between the ages of fifteen and twenty-nine, homicides is the number one cause of black men's deaths.
- Seventy percent of all black children are born out of wedlock.
- Seventy percent of all black households are without a male parent.
- Statistic show 43.1 percent of all black males are unemployed.

- Seventy-five percent of all black males are either: underemployed, unemployed, or unemployable.
- Thirty-three percent of all black people are members of the permanent underclass.
- The black infant mortality rate is 13.2 percent deaths per one thousand live births; it is 5.6 percent for whites.
- Fifty percent of all prisoners have a child under the age of eighteen.

The United States has 2.3 million people behind bars, almost one of every one hundred Americans, according to the *New York Times,* and one in nine black children has a parent in jail. It is not morally and ethically fair to scrutinize, ostracize, and victimize their children. Yet the US Constitution enforced by the three branches of the government (the legislative branch, the US Supreme Court, and the executive branch) continue to make laws that avoid adequate education, health care (the parents must also have health care, including dental), and adequate jobs. Black males born 2001 have a 32 percent chance of spending time in prison at some point in their lives. A Hispanic male has a 17 percent chance, and a white male has a 6 percent chance of spending time in prison at some point in his life.

Several states pay $60,000 a year or more to incarcerate one person; nearly 95 percent are eventually released back into society (www.prisoncommission.org/report.asp) ill-equipped to lead productive lives. Within three years, 67 percent are rearrested, and 52 percent are re-incarcerated. This recidivism rate calls into question the effectiveness of American's correctional institutions, which cost taxpayers $60 billion a year.

In 1972, the prison and jail population nationwide was approximately three hundred and fifty thousand people. "The National Advisory Commission of Criminal Justice Standards and Goals in 1973 recommended that no new institutions for adults should be built and existing institutions for juveniles should be closed" *(New Jim Crow,* 8).

In metropolitan areas in 1970, over 70 percent of Negroes held blue-collar jobs *(New Jim Crow,* 50). The economy sputtered during

1970, and millions of workers lost high-paying industrial jobs as the Industrial Revolution ended. The least-skilled and least-educated workers were the first to go. "Middle management and lower-level workers who had little hope of getting their jobs back scrambled for work as millions of women entered the labor force to help maintain family incomes" *(American Labor BSA,* 21, 23). The ill-equipped African American needed to be trained in: 1) new mind-sets; 2) new skill-sets; and 3) new tool-sets.

In the 1980s and 1990s, the semiconductor, microchip, personal computers, global communications satellites, and Internet required workers who understood technology. Globalization and deindustrialization is the culprit of the inner city black communities; during that period, black men's employment fell to 28 percent, and people had to lean on the Social Service System. And to make matters worse, in 1985 after Reagan declared a War on Drugs in 1982, crack cocaine hit the streets. This led to extreme violence as drug markets struggled to stabilize and as anger and frustration associated with joblessness boiled *(The New Jim Crow,* 50).

Social Service System

The single parent on welfare has enough problems trying to raise children alone. Many usually have no vision of escaping their poverty condition. Humiliated by their case workers over small technicalities, they lose their food stamps, cash assistance, housing, and medical benefits. This creates stress not only on the parent but also on the child. Many times the parent must choose to go to the welfare office rather than reporting for work. If the parent receives a slight increase in wages, the rent increases and the food stamps decrease. Many would argue, "Why didn't they think of these things before they had the children, or why didn't they do family planning? In Exodus 1:8—14, we see that when people are persecuted, afflicted, and oppressed, they will multiply. The sad part about this is that the multiplying will continue until they discover their destiny. The two greatest days in people's lives are the day they are born and the day they discover why they were born.

Welfare took on a new face under the Clinton administration, creating the current paternalistic caste system. The Personal Responsibility and Work Opportunity Reconciliation Act was an insensitive act. It did not take in consideration the person's learning skills and the market's need. The US House of Representatives knew globalization was the result of corporations' disputes with the labor unions and labor unions' corruption. It also knew that for low-skilled workers, a new mind-set, a new skill-set, and a new tool-set was mandatory. Living in ghetto communities of high crime and attending low-performing schools did not lend itself to focus on personal development. They were not taught and educated on assessing their values, interest, abilities, and skills. Many people are on welfare because they have not seen value in a future career or discovered their innate abilities and interests.

The Family Need Analysis

What the federal government should have done was to do a complete need analysis on all applying for welfare, including a career interest survey. This would allow them to be placed on a career path. Instead, this act immediately led the crack prostitutes, welfare queens, and gangbangers to centers that taught them to create an effective resume. A resume is an essential document that helps people highlight their education, work experience, awards, professional memberships, colleges, and community activities. These individuals had not grown up in a positive environment where character was practiced, such as: respect, responsibility, perseverance, honesty, trust, care, fairness, and citizenship, courage, and life skills.

Abilities and characteristics are core values that a high-tech and critical-thinking workforce seeks. To be successful in the information/ technology and wisdom age, an employee must be constantly developing in communication skills, intellectual ability, integrity, personal motivation, initiative, ability to work independently, responsibility, reliability, leadership potentials, interpersonal skills, quality of relationships, emotional stability and the ability to handle stress, sensitivity, and empathy.

From the Personal Responsibility and Work Opportunity Reconciliation Act came the Temporary Assistance to Needy Families block grant to each state, imposing "a five-year lifetime on welfare assistance, as well as a permanent, lifetime ban on eligibility for food stamps for anyone convicted of a felony drug offence—including simple possession of marijuana" *(The New Jim Crow, 56)*. Because of government ineptness and treachery, the socioeconomically disadvantaged, at-risk people are manipulated by the social service system rather than it being their voice. Their lack of effective services also contributes to wasteful spending. The social service system is designed to address poverty. And to address poverty, one must be holistic in one's approach and not a Band-Aid over a missile wound.

The At-Risk (Pariah) Family

A range of risk factors, including chronic stress, unemployment, and poor mental health, are associated with low socioeconomic status. Poverty has profound effects on the psychological development and mental health of children. The indirect consequences of poverty are often invisible within the homes and may challenge marital and parent-child relationships, and sometimes altering a parent's ability to nurture and parent responsibly. Each new generation finds itself lacking the emotional and social tools necessary to nurture its offspring; these parents will be the least likely to promote cognitive development in their homes. They give little attention to their children, give negative feedback, use commands, and will be less likely to praise them. This child is at-risk for low academic achievement, which often leads to future behavioral and motivational Problems.

Homelessness

Homelessness is defined as "having no shelter, living in shelters or missions, living as transients in cheap hotels or rooming houses, or staying with family or friends on temporary basis"

(Baker's Encyclopedia of Psychology & Counseling, 891). One-third of the homeless population is suffering from severe mental illness, including schizophrenia, bipolar disorder, or severe depression, and 35 percent to 40 percent use drugs and alcohol. Poverty, whether in a child, youth, or an adult, will wreak havoc on mental health.

The social service system should not be the only effective voice for the poor, but the Christian church should be as well. Jesus calls Christians to respond empathically, materially, and spiritually.

> If you wish to be perfect, go, sell your possessions, and give the money to the poor, and you will have treasures in heaven; then come, follow Me. (Matt. 19:21 NRSV)

> But when you give a banquet, invite the poor, crippled, the lame, and the blind. And you will be blessed, because they cannot repay you, for you will be repaid at the resurrection of the righteous. (Luke 14:13 NRSV)

James, the brother of Jesus, articulates forcefully the sin of ignoring the poor:

> Listen, my beloved brothers and sisters. Has not God chosen the poor in the world to be rich in faith and be heirs of the kingdom that He has promised to those who love Him? But you have dishonored the poor. (James 2:5-6 NRSV)

Poor parents, children, and the homeless need resources, skills, food, and clothes. Yet they need so much more; they need hope and support. Hope brings vision, a plan for the future, and the belief that one can make it despite incredible barriers.

The Family

Parents have numerous responsibilities in a child's development. When basic principles of authority and self-discipline are not caught early in a child's life, the child often rejects all forms of authority as a teenager and young adult. However, if a child learns to obey his or her parents and understand the principles of authority, he or she is prepared to respect all other authorities in life, including those appointed over him or her, such as teachers, police, work supervisors, and the military. National disintegration begins in the family.

- Insecure husbands result in insecure wives.
- Insecure wives result in insecure children.
- Insecure children produce an insecure generation.
- An insecure generation demands security.
- In demanding security from government, an insecure generation becomes an entitlement generation.
- Entitlements are offered to an insecure generation by politicians.
- Insecure politicians offer some form of socialism that is always divorced from established principles found in the infallible Word of God.

There are many risk factors in African Americans' lives today that are deeply rooted in the legacy of slavery and racism that have enormously shaped the quality of life and conditions for generations to come. Out of slavery the African discovered true Christianity and that this world is the Devil's world. Christians are those who trust in Jesus and after death, live with Christ forever. Evildoers will burn in the lake of fire with Satan and his angels.

SECTION 3

SATAN VS. GOD

(SCRIPTURE OF THE ANGELIC CONFLICT)

AFRICAN-AMERICAN LIBERATION THEOLOGY

The Prince of Darkness

Before the creation of humankind, God created a vast angelic host, unseen today but real. "Everything was created by Him, everything in heaven and on earth, everything seen and unseen, including all forces and powers, and all rulers and authorities" (Coiossians 1:16). The preeminent angel was Lucifer, the bright morning star (Isaiah 14:12), the most dazzling creature of light ever to come from the hand of God: 1) his radiant beauty breathtaking in its perfection; 2) his voice resonant and melodious; 3) his wisdom beyond mortal comprehension; and 4) his clothing of iridescent light, studded with priceless Jewels. God appointed this peerless angel to the exalted position of honor guard of His throne *(Satan and Demonism,* 1). "At one time you were perfect, intelligent, and good looking. You lived in the Garden of Eden, and you wore Jewelry made of Bright-colored gems, and precious stones ..(Ezekiel 28:12b—15)

Lucifer should have responded to this supreme honor and privilege with devotion to his Creator.

Instead, he became narcissistic and enamored with his importance. His brilliance and beauty ignited arrogance and a flame for power. He craved to possess the very power and glory of God *(Jhe Angelic Conflict,* 3-12). "You said to yourself, I'll climb the heavens and place my throne above the highest stars. I'll sit there with others gods far away in the north. I'll bed above the clouds, Just like God Most High" (Isaiah 14:13—14). Jesus said in Luke 10:18 to His disciples, "I saw Satan fall from heaven like a flash of lightning."

Satan's Trial

In eternity past, God the Judge and Prosecutor convened a trial to judge the defiant angels. Satan was the defense attorney for himself and the fallen angels; they were pronounced guilty and condemned to spend eternity in the lake of fire. Jesus said in Matthew 25:41, "Then the King will say to those on His left, 'get away from Me! You are under God's curse. Go into the everlasting fire prepared for the devil and his angels." In Revelation 20:10, John said, "Then the devil that fooled them will be thrown into the lake of fire and burning sulphur. He will be there with the beast and the false prophets, and they will be in pain day and night forever and ever." Lucifer's new title is Satan, meaning "adversary, accuser." This is best described in Zechariah 3:1b—2b, "This time Joshua the high priest was standing in front of the Lord's angel. And there was Satan, standing at Joshua's right side, ready co accuse him. But the Lord said, 'Satan, you are wrong" ("The angels are members of God's Council, who stand beside the throne of God in heaven and are allowed to speak with Him and for Him" The Bible, CEV, 965). Satan lodged an appeal at the conclusion of his trial, questioning the character of God: How could a loving God cast His creatures into the lake of fire *(Christian Suffering,* 158—71)?

The Proposal of Human Creation

- The human race was created to resolve Satan's appeal. "Through humankind God will display His perfect justice. Like the angels, humankind has been endowed with volition, the freedom to choose for or against God" *(Satan and Demonism,* 3). Humanity's first encounter with Satan was in the Garden of Eden as he spoke to Eve through the serpent (Genesis 3:1-5) as they visited the forbidden Tree of Knowledge of Good and Evil. The Tree of Knowledge of Good and Evil embodied Satan's plan; it is the sum total of Satan's policy for ruling the world. Evil is the sum total of his genius. Satan sponsors many different ideas and false systems of thought. His purpose is to gain control of the human souls of the entire human race:

- "Out of your heart come evil thoughts, murder, and unfaithfulness in marriage, vulgar deeds, stealing, telling lies, and insulting others" (Matthew 15:9).
- "God's Spirit clearly says that in the last days many people will turn from their faith. They will be fooled by evil spirits and by teachings that come from demons" (1 Timothy 4:1).

Evil thinking leads to evil function. "Adam rejected God's provisions in the Garden, decided instead to eat from the tree of knowledge of Satan's plan—good and evil—and plunged the entire human race into spiritual death under Satan's new regime" (*The Integrity of God,* 54). Since Satan usurped the earthly throne from Adam, every person born (except the virgin-born Jesus Christ) is a natural citizen of the Devil's regime.

Paul says in Ephesians 6:12, "We are not fighting against humans. We are fighting against forces and authorities and against rulers of darkness and powers in the spiritual world." The spiritual world is the soul. The soul is a person's essence: self-awareness, mentality, consciousness, and volition (free will). Jesus said in John 10:10, "The thief comes only to rob, kill, and destroy." In John 8:44, Jesus said, "The devil ... has always been a murderer and a liar. There is nothing truthful about him. He speaks on his own, and everything he says is a lie. Not only is he a liar himself. He is also the father of all lies."

Through the snake in Genesis 3, Satan convinced Adam and Eve to commit the first sin. Verse lb says, "Did God tells you not to eat fruit from any tree in the garden?" In verses 2—3, the woman replied, "God said we could eat fruit from any tree in the garden, except the one in the middle. He told us not to eat fruit from that tree or even to tough it. If we do, we will die." In verses 4-5, the snake responded, "No, you won't! God understands what will happen on the day you eat fruit from the tree. You will see what you have done, and you will know the difference between right and wrong, just as God does." Adam and Eve rejected God's plan in favor of Satan's.

Before Eve leaped at the prospect of being smart like God, their point of contact with God was His attribute of love; after being flattered by Satan and attempting to become a free spirit, Eve and Adam died spiritually, and the attribute of justice became their point of contract and also for their progeny. Love allowed them to fellowship with God; justice required them to be expelled from the garden. God's grace and mercy were activated. Grace is God's unmerited favor; mercy is God's continuous grace in action.

> As the appeal trial of Satan unfolds, the grace of God and the perfect justice of His verdict are proven again and again. God introduces changes into His administration of human history in order to present His case, disprove Satan's case, and deliver a decisive closing argument. These changes produce the dispensations. (*The Divine Outline History*, 7)

The Satanic system pervades every aspect of life for every human in the world. In America, many people's lives are being destroyed in the name of "the greatest good for the greatest number." Since Adam and Eve failed to recognize Satan's cynical innuendoes as anti-God, justice is the point of contact through every dispensation.

Divine Dispensation of Human History

> A Dispensation is a period of human history defined in terms of divine revelation. According to the Bible, history is a sequence of divine administrations. These consecutive eras reflect the unfolding of God's plan for humankind. The doctrine of dispensations is the vehicle by which believes living at a specific time can orient to God's will, plan, and purpose for their lives. (*The Divine Outline of History*, 3)

From the creation of humanity to the final judgment, there exist six dispensations, which are grouped into three categories. Each category involves two dispensations *(The Divine Outline of History)*:

1. Theocentric (Age of the Gentiles and Age of Israel)
2. Christocentric (Hypostatic Union and the Church Age)
3. Eschatological (Tribulation and Millennium)

Theocentric is defined as having God as the central interest and ultimate concern. The book of Genesis addresses the Age of Gentiles. Genesis 1—11 tells about creation and the human race up to Abraham; the rest of the book contains the story of Abram and his family. The book of Exodus beings the Age of Israel and continues through the book of Malachi.

Christocentric is defined as centering theologically on Christ. Hypostatic Union is addressed in the New Testament books of Matthew, Mark, Luke, and John. The Church Age books begin with the book of Acts and conclude with the book of Jude.

Eschatology is defined as the branch of theology concerned with the final events in the history of the world or of humankind. It is a belief concerning death, the end of the world, or the ultimate fate or destiny of humankind. The book of Revelation addresses the tribulation, the millennium, the lake of fire, the new heaven, and the new earth.

Hypostatic Union

The hypostatic union began at Virgin Mary's conception. The angel said to Joseph in a dream, "The baby that Mary will have is from the Holy Spirit. Go ahead and marry her. Then after her baby is born, name Him Jesus, because He will save His people from their sins" (Matthew 1:20-21). In Luke 1:26-33, God sent His angel Gabriel to Nazareth in Galilee to visit a young virgin girl (age thirteen) named Mary. Gabriel said to Mary, "God is pleased with you, and you will have a son. His name will be Jesus. He will be great and will be called the son of God Most High. The Lord God will make Him King, as His ancestor David was. He will rule the people of Israel forever, and His kingdom will never end.

" The Holy Spirit fertilized the ovum, which is the only pure, uncontaminated cell in the human body since Adam's original sin in the garden.

> In this normal biological process God made provision to fulfill the promise that Christ, the seed of the woman (Genesis 3:15, the age of the Gentiles), would become the Savior. In female meiosis, God paved the way for the virgin birth by which the Second Person of the Trinity entered the world as perfect, uncontaminated man, qualified to go to the cross as our substitute. *(fhe Integrity of God, 68)*

Adam sinned (by yielding to Satan), and that sin brought death into the world.

In Romans 5:12, Paul said, "Now everyone has sinned, and so everyone must die." In verse 1, he said, "By faith we have been made acceptable to God." During the Age of Israel (from Moses to Hypostatic Union), the prophet Isaiah in 6:14b said, "A virgin is pregnant; she will have a son and name him Immanuel (God is with us)." In Isaiah 9:6—7 he wrote.

> A child has been born for us. We have been given a son who will be our Ruler. His names will be Wonderful Advisor and Mighty God, Eternal Father and Prince of Peace. His power will never end; peace will last forever ... He will always rule with honesty and justice. The Lord All-Powerful will make certain that all of this is done.

Through the virgin birth, "Jesus Christ was truly God. But He did not try to remain equal with God. He gave up everything and became a slave, when He became like one of us" (Philippians 2:6-7).

First Timothy 3;16 says, "Christ came as a human."

The Spirit proved that He pleased God, and He was seen by angels. Therefore, Jesus Christ is fully God and fully man. This is called the hypostatic union, which began at conception and terminated with His death, burial, resurrection, ascension, and session at the right hand of the Father in heaven *(The Divine Outline of History, 39)*.

THE TRINITY

The Godhead

> In the beginning was the one who is called the Word. The Word was with God and was truly God. From the very beginning the Word was with God ... The Word became a human being and lived here with us. We saw His true glory, the glory of the only Son of the Father. From Him all the kindness and all the truth of God have come down to us. (John 1:1—2, 14)
>
> God sent His Son co bring His message CO US. God created the universe by His Son, and everything will someday belong to the Son. God's Son has all the brightness of God's own glory and is like Him in every way. By His own mighty word. He holds the universe together. (Hebrews 1:2—3)
>
> God Himself was please to live fully in His Son. And God was pleased for Him to make peace by sacrificing His blood on the cross, so that all beings in heaven and on earth would be brought back to God. (Colossians 1:19-20)

God is one in essence but three in persons. God is three distinct persons in the Godhead (Trinity): God the Father, God the Son, and God the Holy Spirit. Each person of the Trinity is coequal, coinfinite, and coeternal, with identical eternal attributes (7Z?e *Trinity,* 1). Attributes are those intrinsic qualities that compose the essence of a person. For humanity, the essence of soul is self-awareness, mentality, consciousness, and volition (being free or ability to choose). The finite essence of humanity is developed through the person's lifetime. The attributes of God's essence follow *(The Trinity, 6-15)*:

- God is sovereign. Sovereign God is the Supreme Ruler of the universe and King of the heaven and earth.
- God is absolute righteousness. The righteousness of God is the perfect standard of His essence.
- God's justice is absolute and incorruptible fairness. God treats all his creatures alike, without bias or partiality.
- God is love. God is eternal, unchangeable, perfect love.
- God is eternal life. God is the absolute self-existing one.
- God is omniscience—all knowing—and has always known all things past, present, and future.
- God is omnipresence—all present everywhere at all time.
- God is omnipotence—all powerful. Nothing will be impossible with God.
- God is immutability—unchangeable. He is the same yesterday, today, and forever.
- God is veracity—absolute truth. Jesus said, "I am the way, and the truth, and the life; no one comes to the Father, but through Me" (John 14:6). First John 5:7 says, "The Spirit is the truth.

The Sin Nature

The doctrine of imputation is the framework by which divine integrity blesses humanity since the creation of Adam and Eve. The justice of God imputed *(The Integrity of God, 50—51)*

- soul life to biological life, creating human life at birth;
- Adam's original sin to our sin nature;
- our personal sins to Christ on the cross;
- divine righteousness to us at salvation; and
- Eternal life to the human spirit at the new birth.

Christ entered the world to address our sin nature. When Adam sinned by disobeying God by eating from the tree in the Garden of Eden (Genesis 3:6-8), he lost fellowship with God. This is called spiritual death. Spiritual death is total separation from God and the inability to have a relationship with God. Every person is born physically alive but spiritually dead. Adam's original sin is genetically passed down to all humanity through the male in procreation. The sin nature resides in the cell structure of the human body. The sin nature is also the center of humanity's rebellion toward God and the inner source of temptation, lust, and human good; and it perpetuates Satan's plan.

The temptation to sin is not sin itself; only through volition of yielding to the negative is sin committed. The sin nature is composed of areas of *(Old Sin Nature vs. Holy Spirit^ 3)*

- strength, which generates human good (Isaiah 64:6; Hebrews 6:1);
- weakness, which is the source of temptation for personal sins (Hebrews 12:11);
- trends toward legalism, which is self-righteousness (Romans 7:7);
- antinomianism, which is licentiousness (Galatians 5:19—21); and
- Lust patterns, which are the motivation toward either trend (Ephesians 2:3).
- Strength: We are unfit to worship You; each of our good deeds is merely a filthy rag (Isaiah 64:6).
- Strength: We must try to become mature and start thinking about more than ust the basic things we were taught about Christ. We shouldn't need to keep talking about why we ought to turn from deeds that bring death and why we ought to have faith in God (Hebrews 6:1).
- Weakness: Such a large crowd of witnesses is all around us! So we must get rid of everything that slows us down, especially the sin that just won't let go. And we must be

determined to run the race that is ahead of us (Hebrews 12:11).

- Trends toward legalism: Does this mean the Law is sinful? Certainly not! But if it had not been for the Law, I would not have known what sin is really like. For example, I would not have known what it means to want something that belongs to someone else unless the Law had told me not to do that (Romans 7:7).
- Antinomianism: People's desires make them give-in to immoral ways, filthy thoughts, and shameful deeds. They worship idols, practice witchcraft, hate others, and are hard to get along with. People become jealous, angry, and selfish. They not only argue and cause trouble, but they are also envious. They get drunk, carry on at wild parties, and do other evil things as well. No one who does these things will share in the blessings of God's kingdom (Galatians 5:19-21).
- Lust patterns: Once we were also ruled by the selfish desires of our bodies and minds. We had made God angry, and we were going to be punished like everyone else (Ephesians 2:3).

Personal sins originate through humanity from three categories (*The Plan of God,* 9—10):

- Mental Attitude Sins: pride, jealousy, bitterness, hatred, vindictiveness, implacability, envy, guilt feelings, fear, worry, anxiety, and self-pity
- Sins of the Tongue: maligning, judging, bullying, gossiping, criticizing, and lying
- Overt Sins: murder, adultery, drunkenness, and stealing Paul in the book of Romans 3:10—18, says of both Jews and Gentiles:

No one is acceptable to God ... They have all turned away and are worthless. There isn't one person who does right. Their words are like an open pit, and their tongues are good only for telling lies ... These people quickly become violent. Wherever they go, they leave ruin and destruction ... They don't even fear God.

In Isaiah 1:18—20 says, "The Lord invites all [humanity] to come and talk it over." He says though our "sins are scarlet-red, they will be whiter than snow or wool. If you willingly obey Me, the best crops in the land will be yours. But if you turn against Me, your enemies will kill you. I, the Lord, have spoken." The religious priests, controlled by the sin nature and through negative volition, crucified the Lord Jesus Christ.

JESUS CHRIST THE GOD-MAN

The Cross: Religion vs. Christianity

Christianity is a personal and eternal relationship with the Lord Jesus Christ through faith in His saving works on the cross. Through faith alone in Christ alone in His salvation work, the believer is born again or regenerated. In regeneration, God the Holy Spirit creates in the believer a human spirit into which He imputes eternal life, making him or her spiritually alive. Salvation is the gift of God made available to all humankind only through Jesus Christ's works on the cross.

Religion is Satan's ace trump. Satan has devised religion to blind the mind of humanity to truth. Religion is devised to gain salvation by works; one attempts to please God by his or her personal merits. These people are self-righteous and overwhelmingly proud of their flimsy works of Baptism, church membership, sincerity, keeping the Ten Commandments, and living by the golden-rule, all which is blended into their evil deeds *(King of Kings,* 4-5).

The religious priests, scribes, and the Pharisees made up the Sanhedrin, which was the political and religious organization of Judaism (ibid., 4):

- The chief priest served in various administrative positions under the high priest.
- The high priest was the chief civil and ecclesiastical dignitary among the Jews, the chairman of the Sanhedrin, and the head of political relations with the Roman government.

- The scribes were the Torah or Scripture scholars responsible for the interpretation and teaching of the Mosaic Law.
- The Pharisees were a Jewish religious sect whose strict adherence to the Mosaic Law, augmented by the legalistic oral traditions of the elders, was hypocritical, rigid, and formalistic (Matthew 23).

Covered by a sanctimonious veneer of piety, the Sanhedrin unabashedly and efficiently plotted and secured the death of the God-man Jesus. Annas was deposed as high priest in AD15 by the Romans. Yet to the Jews he was of authority and "engaging in gangster activities connected with every system of graft in Jerusalem and with the bands of robbers in the Negev who owed their protection to him" (ibid, 5). Annas, taking authority over Caiaphas, the high priest, conducted the first of Jesus' six trials and said in effect, "Take Him in and railroad Him through the court!"

"The Father loves Me, because I give up my life, so that I may receive it back again. No one takes My life from Me. i give it willingly! I have the power to give it up and the power to receive it back again, just as My Father commanded Me to do" (John 10:17—18). The Lord Jesus Christ died twice on the cross:

1. He suffered substitutionary "spiritual death" for humanity's sins of past, present, and future for the entire world. He is the Lamb of God who takes away the sin of the world (John 1:29b).
2. He also died physically. His physical death signified that the penalty for sin is paid for, and in three days he must rise from the grave.

Upon His physical death

- His spirit went into the presence of God the Father;
- His soul went into a compartment of Hades known as paradise (Luke 16:22—23); and
- His body went into the grave for three days. On the third day, His body was rejoined by His soul and spirit; both

literally and bodily. He rose from the dead (Matthew 28:9—10; Mark 16:9-10; Luke 24:6-7; John 20:14-17).

> Christ was humble. He obeyed God and even died on a cross. Then God gave Christ the highest place and honored His name above all others. So at the name of Jesus everyone will bow down, those in heaven, on earth, and under the earth. And to the glory of God the Father everyone will openly agree, "Jesus Christ is Lord." (Philippians 2:8-11)
>
> After the Son had washed away our sins. He sat down at the right side of the glorious God in heaven. He had become much greater than the angels, and the name He was given is far greater than any of their. (Hebrews 1:3c-4)

During God the Son's hypostatic union. He would speak from one of three sources: His deity, His hypostatic union, or His humanity *(King of Kings, 38)*.

- From His deity alone: "I and the Father are one" (John 10:30); "The Son of Man has authority on earth to forgive sins" (Matthew 9:6).
- From His hypostatic union: "If you are tired from carrying heavy burdens, come to Me and I will give you rest" (Matthew 11:28); "I am the way, and the truth, and the life; no one come to the Father, but through Me" (John 14:6).
- From His humanity on the cross: "ELI, ELI, LEMA, SABACHTHANI?" that is, "MY GOD, MY GOD, WHY HAVE YOU DESERTED ME?" (Matthew 27:46); "I am thirsty" (John 19:28).

On the cross, the Lord Jesus Christ prayed for His enemies who punched Him, beat Him, spit upon Him, lied about Him, ridiculed Him, and scoured Him. The same ones who cried, "Crucify Him, crucify Him," pushed His cross into the upright position and stood around the cross mocking, laughing, and ridiculing the Savior of the human race. He opened and closed His public ministry with prayer.

- In Luke 3:21, after Jesus Himself was baptized, "He prayed, the sky opened up, and the Holy Spirit came down upon Him in the form of a dove. A voice from heaven said, 'You are My own dear Son, and I am pleased with You.'"
- Jesus closed His ministry with prayer in Luke 23:33—34: "When the soldiers came to the place called 'The Skull,' they nailed Jesus to a cross. They also nailed the two criminals to the crosses, one on each side of Jesus. Jesus said, 'Father, forgive these people! They don't know what they're doing.'"

Because God the Father had to break relationship with Jesus for three hours while Christ bore our sins on the cross, from His humanity He screamed over and over again in unspeakable agony. God poured out on Jesus all past, present, and future sins of every person who ever lived since Adam and for every person who will ever live. In John 19:30, Jesus uttered the words "It is finished." When the Lord Jesus Christ uttered, "It is finished," He was saying salvation is complete forever. By faith alone through Christ alone, nothing can take away salvation; it is purely a matter of grace. Grace is God's unmerited favor, which cannot be earned or deserved; it is God's free gift. Paul says in Ephesians 2:8-9, "You were saved by faith in God, who treats us much better than we deserve. This is God's gift to you, and not anything you have done own your own. It isn't something you have earned, so there is nothing you can brag about."

The Death of Jesus

While Jesus was hanging on the cross before His close friends and the crowd, the sky turned dark from noon until middle of the afternoon. "The sun stopped shining, and the curtain in the temple split down the middle. Jesus shouted, 'Father, I put Myself in your hands!' Then He died" (Luke 23:45--46). There were immediate repercussions at the death of Jesus on the cross. Matthew 27:52-53 says, "Graves opened, and many of God's people were raised to life.

They left their graves, and after Jesus had risen to life, they went into the holy city, where they were seen by many people."

At the moment Christ dismissed His spirit, God Himself split the veil of the temple. God's message was that the sin barrier between humanity and Him was removed by Jesus Christ's work on the cross. By Christ's work of the cross He became the way, the truth, and the life to the Father (John 14:6). Some of the Old Testament believers were resuscitated to function as witnesses for God the Son. "They eventually died and their bodies returned to the grave while their souls and spirits entered into the presence of the Lord" *(King of Kings, 51).*

The Resurrection

After God became man and purchased salvation for all humankind of all dispensations—past, present, and future—by shedding His blood on the cross. He demonstrated His system of power by resurrecting His humanity—Jesus. The God-man "humanity is a guaranty that we have a Savior, a Royal High Priest, a Mediator, and a King—King of kings and Lord of lords who will return to this earth and reign forever and ever!" *(King of Kings, 45)* God the Father awarded Christ His battlefield royalty for defeating Satan in the angelic conflict. "Christ won the strategic victory through His spiritual death, physical death, burial, resurrection, ascension, and session at the hand of God the Father" *(The Integrity of God, 119).*

The Holy Spirit at Pentecost

There are seven salvation ministries of the Holy Spirit *(The Integrity of God, 117 30):*

1. Efficacious Grace: God the Holy Spirit comes to the rescue of the positive unbeliever, making faith in Christ effectual by providing the divine power to produce the intended result and purpose: salvation.

2. Regeneration: At the moment of salvation, the Holy Spirit creates a human spirit in rhe believer in which one receives eternal life.

3. Baptism of the Holy Spirit: At the moment of salvation, God the Holy Spirit places each Church Age believer into union with Christ.

4. Indwelling of the Holy Spirit: God the Holy Spirit at salvation takes up residence in our bodies as temples for Christ to reside and manifest His Glory in our lives and to provide encouragement, motivation, and confidence.

5. Filling of the Holy Spirit: The filling of the Spirit control the soul to provide the power needed to combat the inherited, resident, and continually active sin nature.

6. Sealing of the Spirit: At salvation we are eternally saved and are members of the royal family of God forever.

7. Distribution of Spiritual Gifts: At salvation every Church Age believer receives at least one spiritual gift at the moment of faith in Christ.

The Holy Spirit inaugurated the Church Age in AD 30. Pentecost is a Jewish festival that came fifty days after Passover and celebrated the wheat harvest. Jews later celebrated Pentecost as the time when they were given the Law of Moses (CEV, 1134). At the festival (fifty days after Jesus' ascension, Acts 1:9) while the Lord's followers were together, a mighty wind from heaven filled the room and "they began speaking whatever language the Spirit let them speak" (Acts 2:1-4).

When God created Adam and Eve, they were trichotomous beings, possessing a body, soul, and human spirit. When they sinned, they became dichotomous, possessing only body and soul. Since the fall, every person is born as a dichotomous being— spiritually dead. To become a trichotomous being—spiritually alive—one must be born again or regenerated. The human spirit is acquired through the regeneration ministry of the Holy Spirit to comprehend spiritual of the gospel *(The Trinity, 35)*. Jesus says in

John 4:24, "God is Spirit, and those who worship God must be led by the Spirit to worship Him according to the truth."

Before Jesus' ascension. He issued a decree to all Church Age believers, saying:

> I have been given all authority in heaven and on earth! Go to the people of all nations and make them My disciples. Baptize them in the name of the Father, the Son, and the Holy Spirit, and teach them to do everything I have told you. I will be with you always, even until the end of the world. (Matthew 28:18-20)

The question to the church is, *"Who authorized the church to Quit?"*

After the Lord Jesus Christ ascended into heaven, He sat down at the right hand of God the Father in glorification, and God the Holy Spirit came to glorify Christ on earth through believers. Jesus had to be absent from the earth before the Holy Spirit could begin His ministry of glorification.

God the Holy Spirit is one of the distinct personalities of the one God or the Trinity or the Godhead. The "one" God's other two distinct personalities are God the Father and God the Son. The Trinity can be understood from the phenomenon of light (*The Trinity*, 18):

1. The actinic property is like God the Father, who is neither seen nor felt.
2. The luminiferous property is like God the Son, who is both seen and felt.
3. The calorific property is like God the Holy Spirit, who is felt but not seen.

"Let all things praise the name of the Lord, because they were created at His command. He made them to last forever, and nothing can change what He has done" (Psalm 148:5-6). In eternity past, the Trinity formulated the divine decree. It is defined as "God's eternal, holy, wise, and sovereign purpose, comprehending simultaneously all things that ever were or will be, in their causes, courses, conditions, successions, and relations, and determining their certain futurition" *(The Integrity of God, 297)*.

"'The earth was barren, with no form of life; it was under roaring ocean covered with darkness. But the Spirit of God was moving over the water" (Genesis 1:2). The mighty Spirit of God hovers over creation. He was active in creation, and His creative power continues today. Job 33:4 says, "The Spirit of God made me; the breath of the Almighty give me life." All three members of the Godhead contribute to make salvation a reality. God the Father sent God the Son into world by way of the virgin birth, and God the Holy Spirit would be the agent of Jesus conception.

> The virgin pregnancy was caused by God the Holy Spirit providing twenty-three perfect chromosomes to fertilize Mary's ovum of twenty-three perfect chromosomes, uncontaminated by the sin nature. Consequently, there was no genetically formed sin nature passed down through the male and no imputation of Adam's original sin. *(The Trinity, 21)*

At salvation we are indwelt by all three members of the Trinity (God the Father, John 14:23; Ephesians 1:3,6, 12; God the Son, John 16:13; 17:22; Colossians 1:27; God the holy spirit, 1 Corinthians 3:16; 6:19-20).

- God the father: Jesus replied, "If anyone loves Me, they will obey Me. then my father will love them, and we will come to them and live in them." (John 14:23) "Praise the God and father of our Lord Jesus Christ for the spiritual blessings the Christ has brought us from heaven!" (Ephesians 1:3) "God was very kind to us because of the Son he dearly loves, and so we should praise God." (Ephesians 1:6) "He did this so that we Jews would bring honor to Him and be the first ones to have hope because of Him." (Ephesians 1:12)

- God the Son: "The Spirit shows what is true and will come and guide you into the full truth. The Spirit doesn't speak on His own. He will tell you only what He has heard from Me, and He will let you know what is going to happen." (John 16:13) "I have My followers in the same way that you honored Me, in order that they may be one with each other, just as we are one." (John 17:22) "God did this because he wanted Gentiles to understand his wonderful and glorious mystery. And the mystery is that Christ lives in you, and He is your hope of sharing in God's glory." (Colossians 1:27)
- God the Holy Spirit: "All of you surely know that you are God's temple and that his spirit lives in you." (1 Corinthians 3:16) "You surely know that your body is a temple where the Holy Spirit lives. The Spirit is in you and is a gift from God. You are no longer own. God paid a good price for you. So use your body to honor God." (1 Corinthians 6:19-20)

THE CHURCH AGE BELIEVER

Pentecost

'The Church Age began on the day of Pentecost, and will terminate when the church is resurrected or raptured *(The Divine Outline of History, 63—70)*. Every Church Age believer is both a priest and an ambassador. The Lord Jesus Christ is our Royal High Priest who won the strategic victory over the angelic conflict. As priest the believer's function is to win the tactical victory by allowing God to demonstrate His love and integrity in our lives. To receive maximum blessings from God as a priest, one must learn and practice Bible doctrine *(The Integrity of God, 107)*. Christians exist to glorify God by receiving His blessings and to represent Christ in Satan's world.

Salvation

- At the moment of salvation, as priests we represent ourselves toward God and in private before God, devoting ourselves to learning the Word of God, advancing spiritually, and receiving divine blessings. In Christ we are a kingdom of royal priests forever (1 Peter 2:5, 9; Revelation 1:6, 5:10,20:6).
- "And now you are living stones that are being used to build a spiritual house. You are also a group of holy priest, and with the help of Jesus Christ you will offer sacrifices that pleases God ... But, you are God's chosen and special people. You are a group of royal priest and a holy nation. God has brought you out of darkness into this marvelous

light. Now you must tell all the wonderful things that He has done" (1 Peter 2:5, 9).

- "He lets us rule as kings and serve God His Father as priest. To Him be glory and power forever and ever! Amen." "You let them become kings and serve God as priest, and they will rule on earth." "These people are the first to be raised to life, and they are especially blessed and holy. The second death has no power over them. They will be priest for God and Christ will rule with them for a thousand years" (Revelation 1:6, 5:10, 20:6).

Also at the moment of salvation, one is appointed as a spiritual ambassador. As ambassadors, we represent our Savior Jesus Christ in the Devil's kingdom, and we also represent God to humanity in public before the world by interacting with others *(The Integrity of God,* 108). In Romans 10:15b, Paul says, "It is a beautiful sight to see even the feet of someone coming to preach the good news." In verse 14 Paul says, "How can people have faith in the Lord and ask Him to save them, if they have never heard about Him? And how can anyone tell them without being sent by the Lord." The salvation message of faith alone in Christ alone to the individual is, "You will be saved (from the Lake of fire), if you honestly say, 'Jesus is Lord,'" and if you believe with all your heart that God raised Him from death. God will accept you and save you, if you truly believe this and tell it to others" (Romans 10:9-10). It is by grace we are saved

Grace

"Grace is a gift from God and not a quality or virtue that belongs to human beings" *(Baker's Encyclopedia of Psychology,* 517). Believers grasp this grace by faith in Christ. A fruit of God's initiative is faith. It is impossible for one who does not believe to begin to believe without God's help; God's efficacious grace or prevenient grace aids in one's curiosity of the Lord Jesus Christ's birth, death, and Resurrection.

Efficacious Grace

Efficacious grace is the ministry of the Holy Spirit to the unbeliever, making effective non-meritorious faith for eternal salvation (7Z»e *Integrity of God*, 117). An unbeliever is spiritually dead and is totally helpless to attain eternal salvation in his spiritually dead state. "God the Holy Spirit in His matchless grace come to the rescue; He makes the Gospel perspicuous. Then He makes faith in Christ effectual by providing the divine power to produce the intended result and purpose—salvation" (ibid., 117). Through faith alone in Christ alone the expression of God is made real and concrete.

Grace is a way of life that stands against any human endeavor to win or to earn God's mercy. Nothing can obstruct that grace to humans (Romans 8) or subvert God's reconciling intervention on our behalf (1 Corinthians 15:20-28). In the end, every eye shall see God (Revelation 1:7), every knee shall bow to God, and every tongue shall confess God, to the glory of God (Romans 14:11; Philippians 2:10-11).

- Romans 8:35: "Can anything separate us from the love of Christ? Can trouble, suffering, and hard times, or hunger and nakedness, or danger and death?"
- First Corinthians 15:28: "After everything is under the power of God's Son, He will put Himself under the power of God, who will put everything under His Son's power. Then God will mean everything to everyone."
- Revelation 1:7: Look! He is coming with the clouds. Everyone will see Him, even the ones who stuck a sword through Him. All people on earth will weep because of Him. Yes, it will happen! Amen."
- Romans 14:11: God says, "I swear by my very life that everyone will kneel down and praise My name!"
- Philippians 2:10-11: "So at the name of Jesus everyone will bow down, those in heaven, on earth, and under the earth. And to the glory of God the Father everyone will openly agree, 'Jesus Christ is Lord!'"

As an ambassador, the world is one's parish. Wherever you are, the circumstances are the pulpit. Our vocation is ambassador. Avocation is how we earn our living. It is a subordinate occupation pursued in addition to one's vocation, especially for employment or hobby. In every walk of life, Christians are ambassadors: in business, professions, labor, and circles in which we move; it is in that sphere that we represent Jesus Christ.

ESCHATOLOGY

Eschatology is those future or final events after the resurrection or rapture of the church or royal family of God is completely formed and transferred to heaven *(The Divine Outline of History,* 71). The royal family is composed of the ones who obeyed the Lord Jesus Christ's message and endured. Therefore, the one who is holy and true will protect His believers from the time of testing (tribulation) that everyone in all the world must go through (Revelation 3:10). At the present time, God the Holy Spirit's mysterious power is at work holding Satan back (2 Thessalonians 2:7).

Rapture

Paul writes in 1 Thessalonians 3:15–16c, encouraging the priest/ambassador to continue developing hope in Christ, because:

> When God brings Jesus back again, He will bring with Him all who had faith in Jesus before he/she died. Our Lord Jesus told us that when He comes, we won't go up to meet Him ahead of His followers who have already died. Then those who had faith in Christ before they died will be raised to life. Next, all of us who are still alive will be taken up into the clouds together with the Lord forever.

At the corporate completion of the body of Christ, the resurrection or rapture will take place. Each believer in Christ will exactly like Christ's resurrection body, free from the sin nature, free from good and evil *(The Integrity of God,* 166). The Church A^e believer's real self is the soul and human spirit united with an interim body (Luke

16:19-31) to dwell in heaven with the Lord (2 Corinthians 5:1-6; 1 Thessalonians 5:23). Each individual is fully conscious and is no longer limited by a mortal body, and each person's perceptive ability is enhanced. The person is completely recognizable and perfectly happy *(The Integrity of God,* 167). At the rapture, the dead in Christ will accompany the Lord from heaven to a rendezvous in space above the earth, where they will be joined by the living generation of believers. There they will receive their resurrection bodies (1 Corinthians 15:51—54; 1 Thessalonians 4:14—17). Afterward, Christ will lead His royal procession into heaven to God.

- Lazarus and the Rich Man: "The poor man died, and angels took him to the place of honor next to Abraham. The rich man also died and was buried. He went to hell and was suffering terribly" (Luke 16:22-23).
- Faith in the Lord: "Our bodies are like tents that we live in here on earth. But when these tents are destroyed, we know that God will give each of us a place to live. These homes will not be buildings that someone has made, but they are in heaven and will last forever" (2 Corinthians 5:1).
- "I pray that God, who gives peace, will make you completely holy. And may your spirit, soul and body be kept healthy and faultless until our Lord Jesus Christ returns" (1 Thessalonians 5:23).
- What our bodies will be like: "Not every one of us will die, but we will all be changed. It will happen suddenly, quicker than the blink of an eye. At the sound of the last trumpet the dead will be raised. We will all be changed, so that we will never die again" (1 Corinthians 15:51b—52).
- The Lord's coming: "We believe that Jesus died and was raised to life. We also believe that when God brings Jesus back again, He will bring with Him all who had faith in Jesus before they died ..." (1 Thessalonians 4:14).

At the completion of the Church Age, the interrupted Age of Israel will resume for its final seven years, which is known in eschatology as the tribulation *(The Integrity of God,* 168). Daniel wrote in 9:24, "God has decided for seventy weeks, your people and the holy city must suffer as the price of their sins. Then evil will disappear, and justice will rule forever; the visions and the words of the prophets will come true, and a holy place will be dedicated."

In the Age of Israel (Theocentric Dispensation), the final seven years were interrupted by the Christocentric Dispensation (Hypostatic Union and Church Age). The Age of Israel's final seven years begins at the rapture. They will continue their completion of the final seven years, which is called the tribulation.

Tribulation

The tribulation immediately follows the rapture. The tribulation is a period of seven years. The first three and a half years of human failure will multiply under Satan's administration of a contagion of bad decisions, and a large portion of the earth's population will destroy itself (Revelation 6:1–11). Utopias are masks for coercion, slavery, and violence. For seven years both human and Satan will discover that they cannot create a politically and socially perfect world.

- At the beginning of the last three and a half years, arrogant, scheming, and belligerent Satan is rejected from the courtroom of heaven. As defense counsel he will have enjoyed free access throughout the appeal trial of the angelic conflict (Revelation 12:7—9; Job 1:6; 2:1; Zechariah 3:1).

  During the great tribulation (Matthew 24:21; Revelation 7:14), Satan's purpose will be to eliminate all Jews. "One day, when the angels had gathered around the Lord, and Satan was there with them, the Lord asked, 'Satan, where have you been?'" (Job 1:6).

  "When the angels gathered around the Lord again, Satan was there with them" (Job 2:1).

  "I was given another vision. 'This time Joshua the high priest was standing in front of the Lord's angels. And there was Satan, standing at Joshua's right side, ready to accuse him." (Zechariah 3:1).

war broke out in heaven. Michael and. his angels were fighting against the dragon and its angels. But the dragon lost the battle. It and its angels were forced out of their places in heaven and were thrown down to the earth" (Revelation 12:7-8).

"This will be the worst time of suffering since the beginning of the world, and nothing this terrible will ever happen again" (Matthew 24:21).

""These are the ones who have gone through the great suffering. 'They have washed their robes in the blood of the Lamb and have made them white" (Revelation 7:14).

The Jews are the beneficiaries of God's unconditional covenants to Israel. If no regenerate Jew remained alive, God would not be able to keep His promise; this make God's character flawed. Satan's ploy, if successful, would be grounds for demanding dismissal of all charges against himself and the fallen angels. Satan's utopian kingdom fragment and collapse into chaos during the unprecedented world war. During the Armageddon campaign, Satan's vast human and demonic forces of great political powers will converge on Palestine. A remnant of Jewish believers will fight for their lives against overwhelming odds, and at the last chance of survival, suddenly the Lord Jesus Christ will return to earth and join the battle (*The Divine Outline of History*, 71—74).

The Second Advent

* The Second Advent is the triumphant return of Jesus Christ as King of Kings and Lord of Lords to the earth at the end of the tribulation (Matthew 24:42, 25:13). Upon His return, the Lord will: 1) defeat the world forces arrayed against Israel at Armageddon (Revelation 19:11—16); 2) depose and imprison Satan for a thousand years (Revelation 20:1-3); 3) establish His millennial kingdom with perfect environment,

including Church Age believers who will return and rule and reign with Him (Revelation 5:10, 20:6); 4) resurrect all Old Testament saints and tribulational martyrs (Isaiah 26:19-20; Daniel 12:13; Revelation 20:4); 5) fulfill the unconditional covenants to the restored client nation of Israel (Daniel 9:24); and 6) begin His thousand-year reign (Revelation 20:4) (*fhe Divine Outline of History*, 74-77).

- "So be on your guard! You don't know when your Lord will come" (Matthew 24:42).
- "So, my disciples, always be ready! You don't know the day or the time when all this will happen" (Matthew 25:13).
- "I looked and saw that heaven was open, and a white horse was there. Its rider was called Faithful and True ... The rider wore a robe that was covered with blood, and He was known as 'The Word of God,' ... On the part of the robe that covered   His thigh was written, 'KING OF KINGS AND LORD OF LORDS'" (Revelation 19:11, 13, 16).
- "I saw an angel come down from heaven, carrying the key to the deep pic and a big chain. He chained the dragon for a thousand years. It is that old snake, who is known as the devil and Satan. Ihen the angel threw the dragon into the pit. He locked and sealed it, so that a thousand years would go by before the dragon could fool the nations again. But after that, it would have to be set free for a little while" (Revelation 20:1-3).
- "And with your blood you bought for God people from every tribe, language, nation, and race. You let them become kings and serve God as priest, and they will rule on earth ... These people are the first to be raised to life, and they are especially blessed and holy. The second death has no power over them. They will be priests for God and Christ and will rule with them for a thousand years" (Revelation 5:9-10; 20:5-6).

The purpose of the one thousand-year reign of Christ of earth is not to establish another Garden of Eden. Adam and Eve had no sin nature in the garden. The millennial reign of Jesus Christ beginning with the Second Advent is a time of perfect environment on earth for humankind with a sin nature. Satan is released from prison ai the end of the millennium. He will gather unbelievers to join him in the Gog and Magog revolution against perfect environment (Revelation 20:1-3, 7-9). The release of Satan and his revolution demonstrates that perfect environment is not the solution to the human problems (The Integrity of Gody 291).

Satan Thrown into the Lake of Fire

After being chained in the pit for a thousand years, Satan is released. He will gather his followers and "surround the camp of God's people and the city that His people love. But fire will come down from heaven and destroy the whole army. Then the devil that fooled them will be thrown into the lake of fire and burning sulphur. He will be there with the beast and the false prophets, and they will be in pain day and night forever and ever" (Revelation 20:9-10).

Those who have accepted the Lord Jesus Christ will not stand before the great white throne at the judgment to be judged for their sins. The judgment is for those who have not by faith alone in Christ alone believed that God raised Jesus from the grave. Those who rejected Christ stand on their own merit, and they are judged according to their works, not according to their sins *(King of Kings,* 47). Believers will live eternity with Christ in the "New Heaven and the New Earth" (Revelation 21fF).

> God loved the people of this world so much that He gave His only Son, so chat everyone who has faith in Him will have eternal life and never really die. God did not send His Son into the world to condemn people. He sent Him to save them! No one who has faith in God's Son will be condemned. But everyone who doesn't have faith in Him has already been condemned for not having faith in God's only Son. (John 3:16-18)

AMERICA IS GOD'S CLIENT NATION

There is little wisdom in the way America is governed. A client nation is a national entity in which a certain number of mature Believers have formed pivot sufficient to sustain the nation and through which Jesus Christ controls history and God furthers His plan for humanity. In Exodus 19:5-6, the Lord God's message to His people is, "Now if you will faithfully obey Me, you will be My very own people. The whole world is Mind, but you will be My holy nation and serve Me as priest." God specifically protects His client nation so believers can fulfill the divine mandates of evangelism, custodianship and communication of Bible doctrine, providing a haven for the Jews, and sending missionaries abroad *(Prayer,* 11).

The Lord Jesus Christ controls history in three ways *(The Integrity of God,* 152):

1. Directly through His divine essence
2. Indirectly through our voluntary compliance with the laws of divine establishment
3. Permissively, by allowing Satan and the angelic conflict and negative volition to run their course

God designed the US government to protect individual volition, safeguard privacy and property, and maintain internal tranquility through law enforcement and external security through military preparedness. First Peter 2:13-14 says, "The Lord wants you to obey all human authorities, especially the Emperor, who rules over everyone. You must also obey governors, because they are sent by the Emperor to punish criminals and to praise good citizens." The subjection of every person to the nation's governing authority is mandated in Romans 13:1-7:

> Obey the rulers who have authority over you. Only God can give authority to anyone, and He put these rulers in their places of power. People who oppose the authorities are opposing what God has done, and they will be punished. Rulers are a threat to evil people, not to good people.

America is falling into a state of reversionism. Reversionism is carnality that has intensified to include the trends toward human good and evil. The reversionist is not filled with the Holy Spirit, and fellowship cannot exist when human good and evil dominate the soul. Carnality grieves the Holy Spirit.

- Ephesians 4:30: "Do not make God's Spirit sad. The Spirit makes you sure that someday you will be free from your sins.
- First Thessalonians 5:19—20: "Don't turn away God's Spirit or ignore prophecies. Put everything to the test. Accept what is good and don't have anything to do with evil."

Many key leaders of this nation have chosen to involve in acts of evil, turning away from God's plan, will, and purpose. When belligerent people are placed in high places, their mission is to vanquish and enslave the weak. Such people, as the case with white segregationists/white supremacists and Negro ciassists, have imposed great evil on helpless African Americans and poor whites.

America is compromising the law of divine establishment with revisionism, and evil is becoming the order of the day. As a result. 9/11 was a warning of the divine punitive action this nation will reap if it does not repent. All nations in Satan's world will eventually succumb if they continue both overtly and covertly the practice of evil. God does not assassinate presidents; that is the mentality and works of Satan. He has used white Americans to do his high-profile duties of evil against African Americans.

The US Constitution was designed to limit government to its true biblical functions:

1. Protect freedom.
2. Teach Bible doctrine.
3. Develop missionaries to evangelize the world.

However, for centuries through the American Imperialist mind-set, personal freedom, privacy, and property are the objects of governmental encroachment and attack. And Bible doctrine is diluted or distorted to manipulate and control the minds of people for personal gain, promoting legalism, socialism, and emotionalism.

We don't live in our own world. We share the planet with more than seven billion people. These people stare at the same sky, but they see it from different positions: coral islands, desert dunes, terraced mountains, rain forests, grasslands, and landlocked megacities. The majority of people want the same things: good health, personal security, and freedom to worship as one pleases, speak what one thinks, choose one's lifestyle, and elect righteous leaders.

In the Declaration of Independence, it states the basic rights of people in the United States of America: "That all people are created equal, that they are endowed by their Creator with certain unalienable rights that among these are Life, Liberty, and the pursuit of Happiness." Abraham H. Maslow identified five broad classes of basic, instinctual needs for people *(Baker's Encyclopedia doo Psychology, 724)*:

- The physiological needs, homeostatic in nature: breathing, shelter, sleep, hunger and thirst.
- Safety and security: security of body, health, family, employment, property, freedom from fear and chaos.
- The need for love/belonging: friendship, family, intimacy, structure, order, and law.
- Self-esteem needs: positive self-image, achievement, confidence, independence, recognition, respect of others, and respect by others.

- The need for self-actualization: creativity, spontaneity, morality, lack of prejudice, and acceptance of facts.

Any government that has intentions to oppress a people because of the way they look is an evil government. America has practiced this evil since the sixteenth century against the Negro. Therefore, there is a spiritual indictment against Satan's forces of evil no matter who they may be. How can a person read and study the Bible when he or she is intentionally alienated, isolated, depressed, and oppressed by his or her government? Why will America deny learning resources, such as schools being properly equipped for the ages, because of people's looks? Racism and classism are both evil. Yet, the oppressor studies from the same Bible doctrine. Satan has blinders on their souls. Those who have practiced, are practicing, and will continue practicing such evil and did not and will not repent and accept Jesus Christ as their Savior, their souls will burn in the lake of fire with Satan and his angels through eternity.

The Lord says in 2 Chronicles 7:14, "If My people will humbly pray and turn back to Me and stop sinning, then I will answer them from heaven. I will forgive them and make their land fertile once again." The apple does not fall far from the tree; just as the Europeans attempted to destroy the Jews, so are they attempting to destroy African Americans. Overtly, it was the gas chambers for Jews. For African Americans, it is overtly by way of the corrupt ordinary injustice system and covertly by way of policy and politics. Satan is skilled in his actions of destruction.

Just as God disciplines individual believers because of carnality, so does God discipline nations. There are five progressive stages of punishment, both for disobedient people and nations; each stage becomes increasingly severe *(The Integrity of God, 293)*

1. The First Stage of Punishment: loss of health; decline of agricultural prosperity; terror; fear and death in combat; loss of personal freedom due to negative volition toward Bible doctrine (Leviticus 26:14-17)

2. The Second Stage of Punishment: economic recession and depression; increased personal and individual discipline for continued negative volition in spite of the first warning (Leviticus 26:18-20)

3. The Third Stage of Punishment: violence and breakdown of law and order; cities laid waste (Leviticus 26:21–22)

4. The Fourth Stage of Punishment: military conquest and/or foreign occupation; scarcity of food (reduced to one-tenth of the normal supply); the separation of families (Leviticus 26:23-26)

5. The Fifth Stage of Punishment: destruction of a nation due to maximum rejection of biblical principles (Leviticus 26:27-39)

SECTION 4

KNOWLEDGE OF WORK
TOOLS FOR THE EXODUS
(Preparation for the Liberation
Through Reasoning)

WHY AND STEP, INC.?

The following information is to help us see the reason why there must be a new developmental strategy to elevate people. This strategy may be done in phases. However, a congregation that is interested in holistic evangelism will through the Holy Spirit seek to be empowered to make the person whole. Every person's desire is to be complete. Jesus Christ is the head of the church (the body of believers). If one member of the body is sick, then the complete body is not well. However, the body continues on even when it has a dysfunction but not without seeking help through medication or some form of therapy or minor and even major surgical operation to heal that dysfunction of the not up-to-par body member.

And Step, Inc.'s founder is Rev. Roger W. Baker, a congregation and community development specialist. The history and major successes of the organization are informed by the founder's experience, research, and study of the need of at-risk African-American families in central Texas, north Texas, and Pennsylvania communities of Ambridge and Aliquippa, and Pittsburgh East End communities (East Liberty, Homewood, Homestead, Penn Hills, Wilkinsburg), in collaboration with African-American pastors across the nation.

In 2006, And Step, Inc. began its focus on Wilkinsburg, Pennsylvania. On September 30, 2009, And Step, Inc. received its 501© (3) IRS nonprofit status. To understand Wilkinsburg requires understanding of the East-End communities: Wilkinsburg, South East Homewood, East Hills, and Southwest Penn Hills. In these communities, the crime rate is alarmingly high:

- murders
- forcible rape

- robberies
- aggravated assaults
- burglaries
- motor vehicle thefts
- arsons
- blight and abandoned properties
- students' failing school performance
- high toxic environmental conditions

Many of these crimes are being committed by youth at a very early age (seven and up). These youth are aggressive and angry; many are medicated, homeless, hungry, and having to struggle for survival and raise themselves. They grow up not only in a violent community but also in violent homes with illegal guns, use of drugs, and crime promotion. And many suffer from post-traumatic stress disorder (PTSD), which is continuously ignored by the borough, county, state, and federal governments.

There are over thirty churches/religious entities within Wilkinsburg, Pennsylvania, a one-square-mile borough with a population of 15,900. There is no youth organization or church/religious entity capable of servicing the pariahs, and neither are they interested. These youth and their parents are not cultured or sensitized for these entities.

Baker's Motivation

After completing a twelve-month tour in Vietnam with the 196th Light Infantry Brigade, Baker became an US Army drill sergeant in August 1967. In Fort Sill, Oklahoma, Baker trained 240 soldiers every eight weeks (with one week of preparation for the next cycle) for combat training. It was there that Baker questioned a young male trainee, asking, "How did you get in this man's army?" His response was, "I had a choice, Drill Sergeant. The judge said, 'Go into the army or go to jail!'" Baker remembered saying to himself, "If I could just get to them before they get here, because here I have to put them in jail."

Baker's motivation to develop a strategy to elevate the socioeconomically disadvantaged at-risk children and youth stems from the announcement by President Ronald Reagan in October 1982 about the War on Drugs. By 1985 African-American communities across the nation were devastated by crack cocaine, helped largely by the government policies of the day. The effect of crack cocaine in people and unborn children were far and wide. The Black Methodist Church Renewal (BMCR), which is black pastors nationwide in the United Methodist denomination, experienced declining membership and a work overload. Many lost their effectiveness because of fear.

Youth organizations and religious organizations were not capable of rendering the necessary services, mainly because they were not sensitized to the needs of those being victimized. One theological seminary in 1995–1997 taught that for churches to evangelize the pariah is "risky evangelism, and it is not worthwhile to mess with." Essentially, there was a sense of despair and lack of coherent strategies to address the socioeconomic erosion of these communities.

As a combat-arms retired army drill sergeant who does not believe in defeat, Baker went underground in 1997 to study delivery, focusing on liberation theology and congregation and community development. It was during this time that he was forced through unemployment to unintentionally live among the underclass: murderers, dope and drug dealers, gangsters, prostitutes, shoplifters the underemployed, the unemployed, the homeless, and those running from the law. This difficult time proved to be invaluable in providing a real-life experience in studying family behavior and conditions of children and youth of the at-risk or pariahs.

Negative Educators

How can European Americans teach African-American socioeconomically disadvantaged, at-risk people when they were taught and are still being taught that African Americans are three fifths of a human being and are "not worthwhile to mess with?" This view was being taught by a seminary in Pittsburgh, Pennsylvania in 1995 through 1997. It is by experience and observation that the state public school system, which is controlled by the union, has a goal to destroy black children and get the pressure off white children for future employment. Many European Americans who are involved in carrying out this mission have a church affiliation. How many children's and youths minds have been and are being destroyed because of this treachery? How many mothers have wept and are weeping over welted over their child's treatment helplessly? What about health costs? What about the prison populations and costs? The US government is guilty of murder and genocide, and Ronald Reagan's administration was African Americans' Adolf Hitler. It is painful to know that the tradition continues both overtly and covertly through policy and politics.

We Are a Reflection of the Past

We only get one chance to prepare our children for a future no human being can predict. What are we going to do with that one chance? If we treat all children and youth as if they are gifted and we always look at them through that lens as being gifted in at least some aspect, they will rise to that level of expectation; otherwise, it is identity theft.

What the world must understand is that no one can force change on anyone; it has to be experienced. Unless we invent ways whereby paradigm shifts can be experienced by large numbers of people, then change remains a myth. People change their capacity for action by experiencing themselves as a part of a whole. We cannot have change without tackling something new. Because the ego-tripping powers resist the unfamiliar because they have a lack of control, a desirable, sustainable, and equitable community is not a reality for the at-risk.

A child is a person who is going to carry on what we have started, be it racist, classist, or one filled with the love of Jesus Christ. He/she is going to sit where we are sitting, and when we are gone, today's children will attend to the things we think are most important. We may create all the policies we please, but how they are carried out depends on our children. They will assume control of our cities, states, and nation. They are going to move in and take over our churches, schools, universities, and corporations; the fate and destiny of humanity are in their hands.

In today's realities, with the wisdom of tomorrow's challenges, we must expose our children from birth to character, leadership, and entrepreneurship principles to turn their vision into reality and their dreams into facts. This requires the community to promote and live a life of principles.

PRINCIPLES, NATURAL AND MORAL AUTHORITY

Natural Authority

Natural authority is the dominion of natural laws: 1) you cannot ignore them; and 2) you must operate by them. All actions have consequences. For example, when you pick up one end of the stick, you pick up the other also. If you jump off a ten-story building, you can't change your mind at the fifth story and say, "I'll go back to the starting point." Gravity controls the outcome. It is the stamp of nature *(The Eighth Habit, 48)*.

Nature has also stamped people with the freedom and power to choose, and therefore, they have natural authority or dominion over things. God said in Genesis 1:26, "Now we will make human, and they will be like us. We will let them rule the fish, the birds, and all other living creatures." Endangered species don't have freedom and power to choose (volition) because they lack self-awareness. Because humans are self-aware, we have freedom and power to choose and to reinvent ourselves. This is natural authority.

Moral Authority

Moral authority is the principled use of freedom and power to choose. If we follow principles in our relationships with each other, then we will tap into the permission of nature. Natural laws and principles control the consequences of our choices. Natural laws are like gravity. Character traits are an outgrowth of principles: of respect, responsibility, perseverance, truth, honesty, caring, fairness, and courage, integrity, self-discipline, citizenship, and life skills. By the principled use of freedom and power, the humble person obtains moral authority with people, cultures, organizations, and entire societies.

Values and Principles

Values are social norms. They are personal, emotional, subjective, and arguable. Values must be based on principles. Principles are also natural laws. They are impersonal, factual, objective, and self-evident. Consequences are governed by principles, and behavior is governed by values; therefore, we must value principles.

Moral authority requires the sacrifice of short-term selfish interests and courage in subordinating social values to principles; our conscience is the repository of the principles. The law of the harvest teaches that principles produce in sequence lasting results and are governed and grow from the inside out. There is a law of the harvest that governs human character, human greatness, and all human relationships; that law is the love of the Lord and Savior Jesus Christ.

Through the And Step, Inc. "Train-Up a Child" nurturing/mentoring model, the staff training to develop the at-risk family must use sensitivity, empathy, and love. They must also have an understanding of the sin nature and the essence of God, and over 80 percent of the at-risk will be delivered in fifteen to twenty years.

Building a Family Foundation

Family Budget

A budget is an estimate of revenue and expenditures for a specified period. Of the many kinds of budgets, a cash budget shows cash flow, an expense budget shows projected expenditures, and a capital budget shows anticipated capital outlays. The term refers to a preliminary financial plan. In a balanced budget, revenue covers expenditures *(Dictionary of Finance and Investment, 83)*.

Monthly Income and Expense Sheet

Monthly Income

Head of Household Net Income $_____ Total Monthly Income $_____ Spouse/Second Net Income $_____ (from left) Extra Income (bonus/etc.) $_____ Total Monthly Expense -$_____ Pension/Social Security $_____ (from below) Alimony $_____ Credit Card/Medical Debt -$_____ Child Support $_____ (see Debt Summary From) Second Job $_____ Other (gifts, inheritance) $_____ Total Monthly Amount = $_____ Total Monthly Income $_____ (funds left over)

Monthly Expenses

Tithe/Offering*** $_____

Savings

Savings/Emergency Fund $_____
College Fund $_____
Retirement Funds $_____

Housing and Living Expenses

Mortgage/Rent $_____
Lot Rent $_____
Homeowner/Renter Insurance $_____
Property Taxes $_____
Homeowner's Association $_____
Security Systems $_____
House Repair/Maintenance $_____
Heating Gas or Oil $_____
Electricity $_____
Water/Sewage $_____
Trash Collection $_____

Telephone $_____

Cell Phone $_____

Cable TV $_____

Internet Service $_____

Pest Control $_____

Pool Supplies $_____

Lawn Care $_____

Insurance

Health Insurance   _____

Life Insurance $_____

Disability Insurance $_____

Secured Loan/Second Mortgage $_____

Clothes

Clothing/Diapers $_____

Dry Cleaning $_____

Auto

Car Payment $_____

Car Payment $_____

Car Insurance $_____

Gasoline Cost $_____

Car Repairs/Maintenance $_____

Auto Tags $_____

Food

Food/Household Expenses $_____

Work/School Lunches $_____

Beauty Supplies $_____

Pet Food $_____

Medical and Health

Medical/Doctor Visits $_____
Dentist/Orthodontist $_____
Eye Care $_____
Medications/Vitamins $_____
Gym Membership $_____

Recreation Miscellaneous and Child Care

Recreation/ $_____   Child Care Fees $_____
Fun Money
Allowances $_____   Alimony/Child Support $_____
Hobbies/ $_____   Private or Home School $_____
Sports/Clubs
Vacations $_____
Recreation $_____   **Total Monthly Expenses: $_____**
Vehicles

Special Debts

Secured Loan $_____
Student Loan $_____
IRS-back taxes $_____

Family Mission Statement

Benjamin Franklin said, "We stand at the crossroads, each minute, each hour, each day, making choices. We choose the thoughts we allow ourselves to perform. Each choice is made in the context of whatever value system we've selected to govern our lives. In selecting that value system, we are, in a very real way, making the most important choice we will ever make" *(The 7 Habits of Highly Effective Families* p.105).

A family mission statement will drive you to do the inner work you need to do to have your own vision and values clear. It provides strength and direction for every configuration: two -parent families, single-parent families, and blended families. Also, it can provide purpose and strength to relationships in the extended and intergenerational family in-laws and children, etc.). Through a family mission statement, you can let your children know you are totally committed to them and you have been from the very moment of their birth or adoption. The power of the family mission statement is that it literally becomes the DNA of the family life. Following are line-by-line examples of a family mission statements (ibid. 92):

- Our family is happy and has fun together.
- We all feel secure and feel a sense of belonging.
- We support each other fully in our seen and unseen potential.
- We show unconditional love in our family and inspiration for each other.
- We are family where we can continually grow in mental, physical, social/emotional, and spiritual ways.
- We discuss and discover all aspects of life.
- We nurture all life forms and protect the environment.
- We are a family that serves each other and the community.
- We are a family of cleanliness and order.
- We believe diversity of race and culture is a gift.
- We appreciate the grace of God.
- We hope to leave a legacy of the strength and importance of families.

For the mission statement to serve as a unifying and motivating influence, every family member's ideas are important when formulating it. Ask questions that will help family members engage all their unique human gifts, such as (ibid. 89):

- What is the purpose of our family?
- What kind of family do we want to be?
- What kind of things do we want to do?
- What kind of feeling do we want to have in our home?
- What kinds of relationships do we want to have with one another?
- How do we want to treat one another and speak to one another?
- What things are truly important to us as a family?
- What are our family's highest-priority goals?
- What are the unique talents, gifts, and abilities of family members?
- What are our responsibilities as family members?
- What are the principles and guidelines we want our family to follow?
- Who are our heroes?
- What is it about our heroes that we like and would like to emulate?
- What families inspire us, and why do we admire them?
- How can we contribute to society as a family and become more service-oriented?

Parent (Mother/Father) Questionnaire

A. Family History

1. Male Name: First _____ Middle _____
   Last _____
   Female Name: First_____Middle_____
   Last _____
2. Address: Street _____
   Apt. _____ City _____
   State _____ Zip_____
3. Telephone (_____) _____ - _____
   Cell (_____) _____ - _____
4. Male Date of Birth: Month _____ Day_____ Year_____

Female Date of Birth: Month _____ Day _____ Year_____

5. Family: Children Name (s)   Age

    _____   _____

    _____   _____

    _____   _____

    _____   _____

    _____   _____

6. Are you presently carrying a child? Yes_____ No _____
7. If yes, month baby is due _____
8. Are you under the care of Health Start? Yes _____ No _____
9. Are you on the WIC program? Yes _____ No _____
10. Will you enroll in And Step, Inc. Parent as Teachers for ageszero to three? Yes _____No _____
11. Will you enroll in And Step, Inc. HIPPY (Home Instruction Program for Pre-School Youngster) for age's three to five? Yes _____No _____

Education:

    Check highest grade completed
    Junior High: What grade _____
    Senior High: What grade _____

    GED: Yes_____ No_____
    If you did not complete high school, would you like to:
    Yes_____No _____
    College Credits Hours: _____
    College Major: _____

Career Related

    What is your professional field of interest?

    _____

    _____

Do you have any training or education in your field of interest? Yes No

Are you seriously ready to seek your educational goal? Yes_____No_____

Will you need transportation to and from child care service while you are at work or attend school? Yes_____ No_____.

Would you work at night if child care service was available: Yes_____ No_____

Psychological Issues

Do you have a faith in God issue? Yes ____ No____

Do you feel that God has abandoned you? Yes____No_____

Would you like to have a mother or father spiritual mentor? Yes_____ No _____

Do you have a mother or father issue? Yes_____No_____

Are you in an abusive relationship? Yes_____ No_____

Do have a child who is troublesome? Yes_____No_____

Have you ever felt like giving up on life? Yes_____No_____

CHILDREN/YOUTH DEVELOPMENT

Grandparents are proud of their grandchildren, and children
should be proud of their parents (Proverbs 17:6)

If parents spend quality time teaching and nurturing their children
in the early years, most likely they will be proud of their children's
success throughout life. There is a saying, "Pay now or pay later."
Spend time training them now, or spend big bucks (dollars) getting
them out of trouble later. Nurture them now, or spend sleepless
nights worrying where they are later. Quality and quantitative
teaching and mentoring a child help him or her enter school with
confidence of being successful.

These children may be white collar professionals if their gifts
and talents are continuously cultivated in their developmental
process. For the black single parent, eighteen years of parenting,
nurturing, mentoring, coaching, and guiding is a long time without
moral and spiritual support. She must depend on Jesus Christ, who
works through the Holy Spirit to guide, counsel, and motivate her
moment by moment.

By observing how the child is developing, she is able to detect
many of the child's areas of interest. The Montessori Method of
exposure helps train the child's senses. During this interaction,
developmental understanding may be obtained about the child.

Basic life skills, such as time management, cleaning the room, and
picking up things and putting them in place without being told should
be taught at the being of understanding, such as: hanging up their
clothes, cleaning their shoes, placing shoes in proper places, washing
dishes, vacuuming the floor, teeth cleansing, bathing, grooming, etc.,
are a few life skills taught at an early age (before age six).

Many at-risk children and youth and young adult parents lack a structural family foundation. Because of the lack of a traditional family background with structure, many are recklessly endangering themselves and other innocent lives. Mainly it is because the home is not the child's first school and institutional base. We must educate future parents that children's first and most influential teachers are their parents. Therefore, the parent must be strong to strengthen the child. The child's strength comes when the parent displays physical, emotional, and intellectual ability in the child's presence.

Most parents have dreams for their children. They want to be good parents, but they need help in identifying their strengths and weaknesses. Confident and competent parents can create a happy, well-rounded, academically able child. The foundation for excellence in education is laid by parents when they promote:

- language and intellectual growth and abilities
- curiosity and social skills development
- problem-solving skills
- Positive relationship with adults.

Infant/child

A baby eventually develops norms and standards through social, academic, and spiritual training *(The Plan of God, 7)*. It has been proven that a child learns more and at a faster pace than at any other time in their lives. For that reason among many others, parents must learn to use many opportunities to develop their child's basic skills, such as: using the correct utensil at meal time, hanging up their coat, placing shoes in proper location, etc. Here the primary intention should be to help the child absorb skills at times when the brain is most receptive to that skill.

It is believed that for every one dollar invested in a child beginning at birth to age five, developing cognitive skills will yield a fifteen dollar return beginning at grade one. Many child psychologists report that between the ages of three and four, the child's brain will grow to nearly three-quarters or between 70 to

80 percent of its adult size. During this time, the child is mastering the most fundamental skills, which he or she will most likely use later in life. By the age of three, the child will absorb and recognize about one thousand words; this is two-thirds of an adult's everyday speaking vocabulary. The child's vocabulary greatly determines the child's ability to reason through conscious thinking. If the child suffers developmental problems, such as language development, motor development, or socialization skill delays, by the time he or she enters kindergarten at age five, it may be difficult to catch up. Early detection may help in empowering the child with a solid foundation of school performance and a life of success.

The Most Important Commandment

In Deuteronomy 6:4–5, Moses says to Israel: "The Lord our God is the only true God! So love the Lord your God with all your heart, soul, and strength." Proverbs 22:6 says, "Teach your children right from wrong, and when they are grown, they will still do right."

The God conscience is a development from birth. "The Train-Up a Child" curriculum Bible study series progresses logically from the concept of salvation and volition to the complex doctrine of the spiritual life:

- Salvation: Spiritual death establishes the need for salvation.
- The Person of Jesus Christ or Christology: In hypostatic union, Christ is the revealed member of the Trinity.
- Essence of God: All three members of the Trinity possess identical essence.
- Spiritual Growth: The Word of God provides the mechanics for living the spiritual life.

The suggested progression from preschool through sixth grade is as follows:

- preschool: volition, life of Christ, Bible verses, Bible heroes, God's grace gifts, and divine establishment

- kindergarten: salvation, life of Christ, Bible heroes, and prayer
- first grade: essence of God, Trinity, life of Jesus, Old Testament doctrines, Old Testament heroes, Abraham, life of David, and faith-rest promises
- Second grade: salvation, life of Christ, life of Moses, book of Jonah, faith-rest promises, Christian soldier, spiritual growth, and New Testament believers
- third grade: forty things at salvation, life of Christ, faith rest promises, life and writings of Paul, dispensations, and canonicity
- fourth grade: life of Christ, winner, faith-rest promises, new species, essence and function of the soul, angelic conflict, divine establishment, national disciple, and the book of Job
- fifth grade: grace, spiritual life of the Church Age, ministry of God the Holy Spirit, mental attitude dynamics, royalty and celebrity ship of Christ, and faith-rest promises
- sixth grade: tabernacle, faith-rest promises, Ephesians, Proverbs, application from Israel, application from David, and application from Daniel

When working with children and youth, one must have a general understanding of their characteristics by age

General Characteristics for Five- to Seven-Year-Olds

- They are eager to learn, are easily fatigued, and have short periods of interest.
- They are self-assertive, boastful, less cooperative, and more competitive.
- They need rest periods. Good quiet activities would be reading books together or doing simple art projects.
- Their large muscles are well developed. Activities involving small muscles will be difficult (working on models with small pieces).
- They may tend to be accident-prone.

- They like organized games and are very concerned about following rules.
- They can be very competitive.
- They are very imaginative and involved in fantasy playing.
- They are self-assertive, aggressive, less cooperative at age seven than at age five, and boastful, and they want to be first.
- They learn best through active participation.
- They are very sensitive to praise and recognition and their feelings are easily hurt.
- They are inconsistent in level of maturity evidenced.
- They regress when tired and are often less mature at home than with outsiders.

The suggested mentoring strategies and opportunities for activities:

- Be patient, encouraging, and flexible.
- Give supervision with a minimum amount of interference.
- Give praise. Bake cookies.
- Visit a playground, park, or zoo.
- Play UNO, checkers, bingo.
- Ride bikes.

The General Characteristics for Eight- to Ten-Year-Olds

- They are interested in people, aware of differences, and willing to give more to others but expect more.
- They are busy, active, full of enthusiasm, accident prone, and interested in money and its value, and they may try too much.
- They are sensitive to criticism, recognize failure, and have a capacity for self-evaluation.
- They are capable of prolonged interest and may make plans on their own.
- They are decisive, dependable, and reasonable and have a strong sense of right and wrong.

- They spend a great of time in talk and discussion and are often outspoken and critical of adults although still dependent on adult approval
- They are very active and need frequent breaks from tasks to do things that are fun for them and use energy.
- They can be very competitive.
- They are choosy about their friends. Boys like boys; girls like girls. Being accepted by friends become quite important. Team games become popular. Worshipping heroes, TV stars, and sports figures is common.
- They are very sensitive to praise and recognition. Their feelings are hurt easily.
- Their idea of fairness becomes a big issue.
- They are eager to answer questions.
- They want more independence but know they need guidance and support
- There are wide discrepancies in their reading ability.

Strategies suggested for nurturing mentors and opportunities for activities:

- Recognize their allegiance to friends and heroes.
- Remind the child of responsibilities in a two-way relationship.
- Offer enjoyable learning experience, it's a great time to teach about different cultures.
- Provide frank answers to questions about upcoming physiological changes.
- Play board games.
- Play miniature golf.
- Play video games.
- Do craft projects and drawing.
- Take them swimming.

General Characteristics for Eleven- to Thirteen-Year-Olds

- They are testing limits and have a know-it-all attitude.
- They are vulnerable and emotionally insecure.
- They have a fear of rejection and experience mood swings.
- Their bodies are going through physical changes that affect personal appearance.
- They are often interested in art, crafts, models, and music.
- They are very concerned with their appearance and very self-conscious about growth.
- Their diets and sleep habits can be bad, which may result in low energy levels.
- Girls may begin menstruation and may begin sexual activity.
- Being accepted by friends becomes quite important.
- Cliques start to develop outside of school.
- Team games become popular.
- Crushes on members of the opposite sex are common.
- Friends set the general rules of behavior.
- They are very concerned about what others say and think of them.
- They have a tendency to manipulate others.
- They are interested in earning their own money.
- They are very sensitive to praise and recognition; their feelings are hurt easily.
- Loud behavior and showing off and hide their lack of self-confidence.
- They tend to be perfectionists. If they try to attempt too much, they may feel frustrated and guilty.
- They want more independence but know they need guidance and support.

Strategies suggested for nurturing mentors and opportunities for activities:

- Offer alternative opinions without being insistent.
- Be accepting of different physical states and emotional changes.
- Give frank answers to question.
- Share aspects of professional life and the rewards of achieving in the world of work.
- Do not tease them about their appearance, clothes, boyfriend/girlfriend, or sexuality.
- Affirm them often. Take them skating.
- Take them to the movies.
- Take them shopping.
- Build a go-cart Take a bicycle trip.
- Play Trivial Pursuit or other board games.

General Characteristics of Fourteen- to Eighteen-Year-Olds

- They are testing limits and have a know-it-all attitude
- They are vulnerable. They emotionally fear rejection and experience mood swings.
- They may identify with an admired adult.
- Their bodies are going through physical changes that affect personal appearance. They are very self-conscious about growth.
- Their diets and sleep habits can be bad, which may result in low energy levels.
- They experience rapid weight gain at beginning of adolescence and have enormous appetites.
- Their friends set the general rules of behavior. They have a fear of ridicule and being unpopular.
- They feel a real need to conform. They dress and behave alike to belong.
- They are very concerned about what others say and think of them.

- They go to extremes. They are emotionally unstable and have know-it-all attitudes.
- They are caught between being children and adults.
- They look at the world more objectively and at adults subjectively and critically.
- They can better understand moral principles.
- Their attention span can be lengthy.
- Argumentative behavior may be part of trying out an opinion.
- They are experiencing romantic or sexual relationships/experimentation.

Strategies suggested for nurturing mentors and opportunities for activities:

- Give choices, and don't be afraid to confront inappropriate behavior.
- Use humor to diffuse testy situations.
- Give positive feedback.
- Be available, and be yourself, with your strengths, weaknesses, and emotions.
- Be honest, and disclose appropriate personal information to build trust.
- Take them to aerobics classes.
- Play tennis with them.
- Take them to skiing lessons.
- Visit ethnic restaurants.
- Take long walks and talks.
- Cook with them.
- Take them to the movies.
- Do community service with them.
- Teach them about car repair.

THE CHURCH'S ROLE IN PARIAH DEVELOPMENT

The church must give both emotional and spiritual support to potential parents. In the black community, we have babies having babies. Why? Sheila R. Staley states the reason like this: "Many children from single-parent households experience their mother rejection, anger, and frustration because they are a constant reminder of her previous bad relationship with their father or of other troubled circumstances" *(The Black Family, 36)*. As a result of their parents' rejection, the male seeks comfort and solace in a gang or in identification with a street man, mainly the neighborhood drug dealer. Sheila further states, "Many young girls attempt to find acceptance and love in an intimate relationship with a man." In other words for both males and females, there is a deep need for love and acceptance, and if they do not find it, they continue to search and drift.

All churches need to be reminded of James 1:27, "Religion that pleases God the Father must be pure and spotless. You must help the needy orphans and widows and not let this world make you evil." Children, youth, and adults of every socioeconomic class should be able to come to church just as they are without one plea. Many of these poor, wretched, and spiritually blind persons are experiencing many conflicts and doubts and are fighting with many fears within and without. They need Jesus. If they are rejected by parents, relatives, community, and the church, where can they turn? Worship calls for community. This Christian community is made up of the body of Christ, and believers have accepted the fact that their sins have been forgiven. It is not by works that we are saved but by the grace of God that was granted on "Evil Friday" and Easter morning. It is being called "Evil Friday" because the sin of humanity manifested itself to the point of crucifying God's Son, Jesus the Christ.

The church is called to minister to single parents and their children. The question is, "Has the church become too heavenly bound to be any earthly good?" The twenty-first-century church must work hard with the guidance of the Holy Spirit in meeting the needs of people; this will enable individuals to vision their future in God's kingdom. To meet the needs of the times, the black church must be in partnership with parents raising their children, learning what and what not to do in perfecting their nurturing and mentoring skills.

The church village must also raise some children and youth. In so doing, the body of Christ is being transformed into the heavenly Father's likeness. God watches over His children. If God guides the eagle through the pathless air, surely God remembers His children. Therefore, the church must develop a comprehensive, community based, intensive, and family-centered plan to change the behaviors of bewildered parents and their children and youth. As African Americans we must take the primary responsibility of solving our own problems by utilizing the resources at hand; then we must seek to subsidize our program by using government and outside institutional resources.

The point to remember is that when we were young, we had bad habits, and many of us were little devils. But it was God's prevenient grace that watched over us and guided us to Jesus. It was the understanding of the working power of the Holy Spirit that enabled us to see our sinful condition. Can the Holy Spirit within its own time frame transform the above individuals into saints of God? We need to remember that God is a forgiving God. He will forgive seventy times seventy times plus more, and each time God forgives, that sin is thrown into the sea of forgetfulness. Yes, He will forgive the gangbanger and the sexually promiscuous girl who had a sexually transmitted disease that caused her baby's death.

THE TRADITIONAL AFRICAN-AMERICAN THEOLOGICAL TASK

Reaching, Bringing, and Teaching

Who authorized you to quit Christianity and revert to religion, black Church? Jesus said:

> I have been given all authority in heaven and on earth! Go to the people of all nations and make them My disciples. Baptize them in the name of the Father, the Son, and the Holy Spirit, and teach them to do everything I have told you. I will be with you always, even until the end of the world. (Matthew 28:18-20)

The African-American church is the strategic and logistical institution in at-risk communities. It is the only strategically based institution black people are able to claim in their neighborhoods. It is the most educational-equipped institution to reach the socioeconomically disadvantaged at-risk people. Yet it is too heavenly bound and self-righteous to be any earthly good. Visit and study the seven letters in Revelation 2 and 3: Ephesus, Smyrna, Pergamum, Thyatira, Sardis, Philadelphia, and Laodicea. Which one or two fit your description? To escape the lake of fire, repent! In Revelation 1:17c-18 Jesus says, "Don't be afraid! I am the first, the last, and the living One. I died, but now I am alive forevermore, and I have the keys to death and the world of the dead."

From the beginning, even the invisible church, black theology was grounded in Christ, "our hope for tomorrow, our rock in a weary land," but since we have been able to obtain some of the goods in the land, many have forgotten God is a forgiving God, a redeeming God, one in whom we should trust at all times. In Isaiah 55:1, the Lord says, "If you are thirsty, come and drink water! If you don't have any money, come eat what you want! Drink wine and milk without paying a cent." In verses 8 and 9, the Lord says, "My thoughts and my ways are not like yours. Just as the heavens are higher than the earth, My thoughts and My ways are higher than yours."

Maximum profit versus life says church seats are needed for those who have money. This is indicated by the space many churches choose for worship. The existing church is saying, "Come in, honey, and join us. In this church we are quiet and orderly in worship. This helps us to cover up our spiritual hollowness, the selfishness and narrowness that perpetuate the status quo. Here Christ is the fairytale hero who rescues our respectability." What they are saying is, "We were here first, and we are not going to change anything. Besides, we pay the bills."

This is a hypocritical attitude filled with false dignity, false pride, and prejudice; in other words, Satan has planted his demons to control. Lyle E. Schaller in his book *Center City Churches* says we need new churches to reach the new generation. For the white churches, this has its financial rewards; but the black churches are experiencing financial difficulties among its members, being the last ones hired and the first ones fired. Many African Americans do not have seniority status within businesses.

Equal opportunity or affirmative action forces businesses to employ at least a small percentage of black. When the firm must lay off temporarily, most likely the African American is the first selected. Therefore, financial security is a problem for many of the black working class. This affects the church's tithes and offering.

Nonetheless, the African-American church must get back into the business of poor people. All black people are at risk; risky evangelism is the thought of the European whites and African American elitists. There is a saying, "Be careful how you treat those while you are going up; you may meet the same ones coming back down." Many children your church chooses to pass up today may be the ones you need when open-heart surgery is an urgent necessity. The time is right for the black church to pressure the government (local, state, and federal) for resources to assist in black community development, making the community desirable, sustainable, and equitable.

To develop the African abandoned and blighted at-risk communities, a twenty-first-century holistic family development institution is mandatory. European Americans cannot teach development to the pariah. The black church must also demand Christian integrity from African-American leaders. There are no abandoned and blighted properties in white communities; only the Negro communities are decimated, and the black (so-called) leadership is content.

This is a changing world. Even though Jesus is the same yesterday, today, and forever, our ideas, thinking, feelings, values, and outlook on life are affected moment by moment in this information/technology and wisdom age. Baby boomers, baby busters, and baby boomlets view God in action differently than the generations of slavery, convict leasing, the civil rights movement, and the War on Drugs. Many parents age fifty and below in the 1980s rejected Jesus Christ because of hopelessness. The slogan went, "God is dead."

- Baby Boomers (born 1946–1964) experienced brokenness and loneliness and became rootless, with a loss of identity and self-seeking.
- Baby Busters (born 1965–1983) were caught in the backwash and received no biblical principles from their parents, leading to a breakdown of family, and materialism became the force.
- Baby Boomlets (born 1984–2002) have very few roots in the African-American culture and identify; therefore, they have become apathetic.

From these pains of the governments and having no "voice" when the serpent was striking violently, hip-hop and New Jack were born out of the aggressiveness of the males for lack of justice (Hip Hop vs. MAAT).

JUST FOR BOYS

The black boy is in trouble. There is no more cotton to pick, tobacco to pull, railroad tracks to lie, or work to do that no one else want to do. Many from birth are not loved by their parents, society, church, or school. Confused and misunderstood, he is placed in special education and drugged with the medication of depression to get him to sit still. Boys never sit still; never did and never will. God created boys to lead and not to follow; he is supposed to hunt and kill. Women cannot raise boys. They can only love boys; it takes an organized man who loves God to raise a boy of character, leadership, and principles by respecting the boy's mother. It is the absence of the black father in the community that has led to at-risk communities. Forced to sell drugs to survive, he must carry a gun to protect himself. Drugs and guns are an indication of rejection by society. Therefore, these boys become the members of a subculture.

Hip-Hop

The hip-hop generation is music centered and rebellious; they are also the urban community's assertive voices. Their language, culture, fashion, and hairstyles shape their identity. They are alienated from Eurocentric dominant culture and from their African-American heritage. They reject the norms and values of the mainstream. For the hip-hop generation, success is measured by peer approval, and they equate power with the ability to influence the subculture. This generation is about change.

New Jack

The New Jack is a new generation of youth following the hip hop generation. The New Jack generation is characterized by new attitudes, behavior, and creative African-American terminology. This is a male-centered culture who feels the need to show disregard for personal safety as a sign of membership. Among the New Jack subculture there is at-risk behavior: substance abuse and promiscuity (sex without planning with many partners indiscriminately). Also, there are high percentage of high school dropouts and functionally illiterates.

There is also a need among the New Jack generation to be a street player and accepted by peers. Many are gang members or potentials. They do not dread death; they will kill to be a member of a society or community. These individuals suffer from antisocial personality disorder.

Antisocial Personality Disorder

Psychopathic and sociopathic personalities are both defined in antisocial personality disorder. The antisocial person is lawless and manipulative and lacks shame and guilt. There is a loss of respect for others' rights and for society. During childhood, there is lying, cheating, stealing, truancy, disobedience, fighting, and running away. For both male and females during adolescence, they will most likely live out destructive behavior and also use drugs and alcohol. Beginning in adulthood, there is usually the inability to establish a permanent marriage relationship or maintain a job, and they will have a growing police record. These individuals are believed to have grown up in volatile homes.

Depression and High School Students

Depression in adolescence frequently co-occurs with other disorders, such as anxiety, disruptive behavior, eating disorders, or substance abuse. It can also lead to increased risk for suicide. Depression is a common but serious mental illness typically marked by sad or anxious feelings. Most students occasionally feel sad or anxious, but these emotions usually pass quickly—within a couple of days. Untreated depression lasts for a long time and interferes with one's day-to-day activities. Different people experience different symptoms of depression. If one is depressed, one may feel: sad, anxious, empty, hopeless, guilty, worthless, helpless, irritable, or restless. Some may experience one or more of the following symptoms:

- loss of interest in activities one use to enjoy
- lack of energy
- problems concentrating, remembering information, or making decisions
- problems falling asleep, staying asleep, or sleeping too much
- loss of appetite or eating too much
- thoughts of suicide or suicide attempts
- aches, pains, headaches, cramps, or digestive problems that do not go away

Any stressful situation may trigger depression. One's environment (surroundings and life experiences) affect one's risk for depression. To feel better when feeling exhausted, helpless, and hopeless, you should do the following.

- engage in mild physical activity or exercise
- participate in activities you used to enjoy
- break up large projects into smaller tasks and do what you can
- spend time with or call your friends and family
- expect mood to improve gradually with treatment
- remember that positive thinking will replace negative thoughts as your depression responds to treatment

If one is in crisis, immediately call 911 or go to a hospital emergency room to get help. Researchers are studying new ways to diagnose and treat depression in high school-age students. Increasing the early detection and treatment of depression can help more students succeed academically and achieve their goals in school and after graduation (The National Institute of Mental Health, handout). Note: Read "Early Adolescence" under "Just for Girls!"

AFRICAN-AMERICAN CHRISTIAN THEOLOGY

America's white Christianity has not reached out to African-American churches in support of the pariah communities. Theology is the study of God and His relationship to the universe through faith, practice, and experience. As Christians, we are called to identify the needs both of individuals and of society. These needs must be addressed out of the resources of Christian faith in a way that is clear, convincing, and effective. It is the church's responsibility to appropriate clearly too every generation God, sin, redemption, and moral and ethical responsibility. If we are to be Christ like, then we are to do the following.

- be our brother's/sister's keeper
- be concerned about humanity's welfare
- Work to increase the population for God's kingdom by decreasing the population destined to the lake of fire.

Those who accept Jesus Christ as their personal Savior are instantly indwelt by the Holy Spirit. From that moment on, the believer is in full-time Christian service as a priest and an ambassador. There are four categories of Christian service *(Prayer,* 10):

- Christian service related to a spiritual gift
- Christian service related to the royal priesthood, which includes prayer, giving, and the execution of the plan of God

- Christian service related to one's royal ambassadorship, which includes evangelism, witnessing, administration in the local church, and functioning in a
- Christian service organization Christian service related to the laws of divine establishment, which includes the family, military service, law enforcement, and government

African-American Male Pastor/Executive Director

A female pastor will not produce effective results of development in the pariah boy. African-American males do not respect female leadership, and neither can women raise a boy. A woman can only teach a boy love. Boys are designed to hunt and kill; girls are designed to love and nurture. The church must seek out and train talented, competent, creative, productive, committed, and visionary full-time black male pastors to administer to the spiritual affairs of the people. They must be learners and active with all people and have a deep passion for the development of at-risk families. They must also be willing to lead their congregations as God leads them.

- The church and pastor must accept the biblical doctrine of R.B. Thieme Jr. Bible Ministries and use it in enhancing spiritual maturity. All members should study and teach this Bible doctrine.
- The pastor must also make a long-term commitment (seven year minimum) to the "Train- Up a Child" nurturing/mentoring model.
- A reasonable and decent financial package must be agreed upon, including housing, utilities, travel allowance, health insurance, vacation, and pension.
- There will be no pastor anniversary that involves financial giving; this is included in the pastor's financial package. The pastor anniversary is designed to make the pastor God, taking the focus off the mission of outreach ministries.

Rather, rally to have a fundraiser for the at-risk in the community for educational travel and exposure.

- Staffing is a necessity; however, teach the youth church administration and give them a stipend. This also includes building maintenance, finances, trustees, church planning, etc. Use adults as nurturing/mentors to develop the leaders of tomorrow.
- Continual education is a priority for the pastor, staff, and all persons in leadership (deacons, pulpit committee, trustees, etc.).
- The congregation members must assume areas of responsibility and support the church's at-risk family outreach programs.
- Prayer is the key. Not the congregation's will but God's will must, be done!
- Every weight that slows one down must be laid aside; the excess baggage must go.

Grief

Grief is the cognitive and emotional process of working through a significant loss. The removal of anything that has emotional value to an individual will precipitate a grief reaction. Grieving is to the emotional system following a loss what healing is to the physical system after surgery. Just as an operation traumatizes the body, a loss jolts the emotional system, producing disruption and upheaval (*Baker's Encyclopedia of Psychology of Counseling*, 519–21).

Abnormal grieving is when a person becomes psychotic and is totally unable to cope. The opposite extreme is to completely disown the pain and proceed with a business-as-usual attitude. Neither reaction is a healthy coping response. Emotional turmoil may lead to wide fluctuations in mood, and feelings of hurt, guilt, depression, helplessness, anger, sadness, love, rage, loneliness, resentment, and hopelessness are the most acute psychological pain. The African American is always in grief because of skin color. And when alienated, isolated, depressed, and oppressed, one develops a sense of hopelessness and may become apathetic.

- spiritless: having or showing little or no feeling or emotion
- indifferent: having little or no interest or concern
- impassive: unsusceptible to pain and physical feeling; insensible

Another goal of the black church in at-risk communities is to recruit a pastor gifted in grief therapy. His purpose is to help the bereaved progressively accommodate the loss and move through the mourning process at his/her own pace. At no time should a black church charge the bereaved family a fee for funeral service; this is a gross church sin. Hosting a funeral service is a church ministry to the at-risk family. By hosting the service, the Lord Jesus Christ is reaching the unreached, bringing the unbrought, and teaching the untaught with the church's cooperation. Therefore, all churches in the at-risk community should make hosting funeral services another one of its priorities. It is an excellent opportunity to introduce the plan of God for life in this angelic conflict. The funeral is designed to promote God and not the goodness of the deceased. We live our funeral, and after death is the judgment.

Organizational Capacity Building

Seek philanthropic-minded individuals who will invest time, expertise, and capital in innovative nonprofits serving at-risk youth and families. Civic-minded individuals can effect positive and lasting changes in the community. They may even engage in hands-on activities, such as the following:

- strategic planning and implementation
- board development
- financial management and planning
- outcome tracking
- effective messaging of project
- technology

To be most effective, key decision makers (the buck stops here; I will get it!) should be the board members and also some youth. They are the ones who want to get it right. Also, the board and church must be deeply rooted in Christian passion and purpose. It will take at least fifteen to twenty years (one at-risk generation) to develop this nation with full cooperation from parents, schools, and all the governmental bodies. The at-risk generation deficit is over seven generations deep.

Following is a holistic family nurturing mentoring model of "Train-Up a Child" in operation by And Step, Inc. Through travel education, this model enriches the child, youth, and adult in regenerative medicine (biotechnology and bioengineering), building architectural/engineering, and SAT preparation through the concept of exposure and practice. We can no longer educate our at-risk children and youth to enter the job market as unprofessional. In many states, the governor determines the prison population by the boy's second-grade school performance. And Step, Inc. purchased a fifteen-passenger E-350 Ford van for the purpose of its vision, mission, and goals.

Vision, Mission, Goals

Vision is seeing a future state with the mind's eye; it is applied imagination. Vision represents desire, dreams, hopes, goals, and plans. They are realities not yet brought into the physical sphere. Mission is the core line of sight strategy. It involves the why, who, what, how, and when. Built into the mission are purpose, vision, and values, with a passionate focus and execution of accountability.

And Step, Inc. has a *vision* of empowering the socioeconomically disadvantaged at-risk children, youth, young adults, and seniors in the Pittsburgh metropolis to be independent, productive members of the citizenry.

The *mission* of And Step, Inc. is to educate and develop this group of at-risk children, youth, young adults, and seniors in the Pittsburgh area by adopting a unique and holistic approach of uplifting the individual psychologically, intellectually, socially, and physically with character building, exposure to leadership, and entrepreneurial principles by way of *travel education.*

Four Goals and Measures of Success:

1. Create a lasting understanding of career opportunities in biomedical fields. Measures of success: At least one student choosing a career in a biomedical field after high school
2. Develop a drive for personal management. Measures of Success: At least one child or adult achieving a sense of responsibility and reliability with a sustaining job.
3. Develop a drive for general self and civic awareness. Measures of Success: Completing the free-enterprise New York City trip, the Shirley ex-Slave Plantation and Washington, DC, trip, and the Freedom Foundation, Valley Forge, Pennsylvania, education trips before completing high school
4. The goal of Family Life is to strengthen the bond between parents and children. Measures of Success: Have a least one family successfully serve as a unit.

SECTION 5

$\backsim\!\!\mathscr{M}\!\!\sim$

USING THE TOOLS FOR PRACTICING DELIVERY
(Experiencing Holistic Development)

TRAIN-UP A CHILD

Character, Leadership, and Entrepreneurial Principles

- The character traits are respect, responsibility, perseverance, trust/honesty, care/fairness, courage, citizenship, self discipline, and life skills.
- Leadership is communicating people's worth and potential so clearly that they come to see it in themselves. When you communicate their potential and create opportunities to develop and use it, you are building on a solid foundation. The four roles of leadership are modeling, path finding, aligning, and empowering *(The Eighth Habit,* 122). In other words, leading is helping others to reach their destiny or goal.
- Entrepreneurship is operating your own business; it is making the best of an opportunity.
- Principles are rules of life; they are universal, timeless, and self-evident.

To assist youth in formulating a vision and mission of the future, we start with present realities.

Working for Minimum Wage as Early as Age Sixteen

On my job I earn minimum wage of $7.15 per hour; I work forty hours a week. I have no health insurance and no retirement other than Social Security. My rent is $550 a month (efficiency apartment all bills paid: gas, light, water, and sewage). A monthly bus pass is $95, and food is $150.

$7.15 (wage per hour) $286 (gross income) $286.00 (gross income) x40 (working hours) 22 percent (Tax deduction) -62.92 (Tax due) $286.00 (gross income) $62.92 Tax due $223.08 (Net weekly Income)

$223.00 net weekly income x 4 weeks = $892.00 monthly income----- $550 rent + $95 bus-pass + $150 food = $795.00 minimum living expenses Money for miscellaneous expenses ------------ $97.00

Nurturing, Mentoring, and Empathy

It is the at-risk children, youth, and adults that And Step, Inc., seeks to engage. These children are engaged from a paradigm of nurturing and mentoring. Nurturing also includes feeding on every event. En route to all events, we stop and order from the McDonald's dollar menu, which is paid for by And Step, Inc.

- Nurturing is the ability to care for and foster growth in oneself and others. At this level we work to engage as many family members as possible.
- A mentor is defined as a trusted counselor, guide, tutor, or coach.
- A Christian mentor is an adult friend in faith and a fellowship friend who is willing to go on a journey of faith with a child, youth, or adult and struggle with him or her to find out what Christian faith (curiosity and principles) and discipleship (character and leadership) are all about
- Empathy is being able to walk in another's shoes and understand another's "essence" as well as to identify feelings and thoughts that dictate that person's behavior.

All staff workers operate in the power of the Holy Spirit. The filling of the Holy Spirit is the enabling power of the spiritual life whereby the believer's soul is under the influence, control, and mentorship of God the Holy Spirit *(King of Kings, 8)*.

The philosophy of nurturing is about encouraging the life force within all living creatures that promotes growth in self and others. It is the single-most-important process for life to flourish in a positive, healthy, and caring manner. Among children, teenagers, and adults, it is the natural ability to care for oneself as well as others in one's environment. Although nurturing is a basic human instinct, the ability to nurture self as well as others can be reinforced or hindered. In the East-End communities and many other communities across America, learning is hindered because of inadequate social, environmental, and economic conditions, and one must also add insensitive policy-making, greed, and politics.

Holistic Family Life Development

And Step, Inc.'s innovative mentoring model of effectiveness stems from the need for a twenty-first century holistic family life development to serve the socioeconomically disadvantaged at risk families in the Pittsburgh region. This approach is absolutely mandatory to sustain the above-mentioned communities. Among the at-risk population is an available, trainable workforce to be developed from infancy through post-high school.

Youth Career Development

The Youth Career Development Department promotes several disciplines but focuses primarily on the following areas:

- regenerative medicine (bioengineering and biotechnology)
- Technology
- architecture and landscape architecture
- automotive and diesel engineering
- Plumbing
- model design and building
- electrical and communication engineering

This after-school model is for children/youth grades kindergarten through twelfth grade. At the present time, regenerative medicine is in operation.

Certified Child Development

From a life-support perspective, included in the institution is a vision of a twenty-four-hour certified child development facility that serves children from birth to independent youth. Also included are several separate babies and children's sick rooms/space for minor illness. There will be a separate children's department for those caught up in family/law enforcement crises. Transportation to and from the institution will be provided for both the after-school and the child development facilities. The working parent's child must be picked up from home one to two hours before he or she leaves for work; the child is returned home one to two hours after the parent returns home. We must work to relieve the pressure and stress of the parent, enabling the parent to increase productivity both at work and at home.

Certified Workforce Development

Additionally, it is the vision that a certified workforce development center be designed to prepare one for career readiness (job placement and continuous monitoring) focusing on both present and future work readiness. In the twenty-first century, the business of America is education. And Step, Inc. understands that nothing is more vital to the competitiveness and advancement of corporations large and small than a literate, tech-capable, and critical-thinking workforce. Also, built into this center is a school-to-work model, which is an opportunity for every youth to be employed in some capacity at age twelve and to mentor. This employment begins the youth's mentor training in an effort to train the youth to teach and share as he or she learns. The thinking behind this strategy is the belief that the best way to get people to learn something is to turn them into teachers. It is only in the doing and the applying that knowledge and understanding are internalized.

High-Quality Early Learning

The "Train-Up a Child" nurturing/mentoring model is designed to promote high-quality early-learning outcomes in multiple domains (cognitive, affective, and psycho-motor) for the at-risk in distressed communities by its complete continuum from the cradle-through school-through-career sustainability. Through travel education, each group of thirteen children (van capacity is fifteen) are age appropriately exposed to the need for social and psychological skills in the development of character, leadership, and entrepreneurial principles. The development of character pervades the very essence of a person, influencing everyday decision making, supporting the essentials of American citizenry, providing open opportunities, and contributing to the rights of everyone.

Regenerative Medicine

On October 11, 2010, And Step, Inc., introduced its at-risk children youth to regenerative medicine at the University Of Pittsburgh School Of Medicine in Scaife Hall. This project is run by Dr. Robert Connamacher, a professor at the university who has dedicated his career and service to increasing the number of underprivileged individuals in medicine. The fall sessions began the last Wednesday and Thursday in September and concluded the week before Christmas (December 25) from 6:00 p.m. to 7:30 p.m. The winter/spring sessions began the second Wednesday or Thursday in January and ended the first week of April.

Major Activities from May 2010 through April 2013

- On Wednesdays from September through December 2010, two medical explorers met for obstetrics and gynecology and surgery on Thursdays. The 2011 winter/spring Thursday sessions were on mental health.

- On Wednesdays from September through December 2011, sixteen medical explorers met for emergency medicine and pathology on Thursdays. The 2012 winter/spring Thursday sessions were on cancer cells.
- On Wednesdays from September through December 2012, sixteen medical explorers met for sexually transmitted diseases and mental disorders on Thursdays. The 2013 winter/spring Thursday sessions were on endocrinology.
- June 17–23, 2012, thirteen medical explorers (six girls and seven boys, grades three through nine) attended the United Methodist seven-day sports camp in Jumonville. On
- August 19, 2012, two youth (president and vice president of youth counsel, age thirteen) attended tissue engineering in regenerative medicine banquet from 9:00 a.m. to 3:00 p.m. at the Sheraton Hotel at Station Square.

Fourteen Medical Explorers registered in January 2013 for the Jumonville Summer Sports Camp on June 16–22, 2013.

Medical Sessions Topics

Following are the topics discussed about sexually transmitted diseases:

- introduction to STDs
- gonorrhea, nongonococcal urethritis
- syphilis
- thrush, candidacies
- AIDS
- herpes, genital warts (papilloma)
- vaginosis, trichomoniasis, pubic lice
- treatment, history, recent problems
- review, slideshow with questions

Mental Disorders Topics

- introduction to mental diseases
- anatomy and physiology of the brain
- neurotransmitters
- depression
- bipolar disorder
- schizophrenia
- strokes concussions, epilepsy
- review of diagnosis and treatment

Endocrinology Topics

- What is it? What causes it? What are they? Disease to be
- Discussed?
- What are major hormones?
- Diabetes I: What is it? What causes it? Toxocities? Blood glucose testing
- diabetes II: Control of insulin production other toxicities, treatment
- Pituitary I: Where is it? How did it get there? Neurohypophysis, adenohypophysis—what do they control and how?
- visit to nursing school
- Pituitary II: What are the effects of hormone production?
- POMS visit
- thyroid and parathyroid glands cancer and treatment, nuclear
- visit to dental laboratory
- growth hormones, male sex hormones
- control of the menstrual cycle, menarche, ovulation and sperm production, menopause
- last day, elections of officers, plan what subjects to be planned for 2013-2014

To attend the 6:00-7:30 p.m. medical sessions, door-to-door pickup must begin at 4:00 p.m. En route to the medical school, the students are treated to a hot McDonald's burger or chicken sandwich and a granola bar. After class they are treated to another granola bar and a candy bar.

Topics are taught every four years; following is a list of topics to be covered:

- cardiology: heart and circulatory systems
- family and preventive medicine
- gastroenterology: problems of liver, stomach, intestines
- genetics: problems with genes, sickle cell anemia
- geriatrics: problems of the elderly
- hematology: blood diseases
- Immunology: diabetes type 1, arthritis, lupus, etc.
- occupational medicine
- ophthalmology: diseases and trauma of the eye
- urinary diseases: kidney and bladder diseases, disposal of waste, hypertension, transplants
- respiratory diseases: lung diseases, pneumonia, emphysema and smoking, cancers
- weight control

Top Thirteen in-Demand Jobs

1. IT jobs of all kinds:1–6 million openings
2. Truck drivers: all types
3. Engineers in all fields
4. Physical therapists
5. Occupational therapists
6. Dentists
7. Physician assistants/nurse practitioners
8. Pharmacists
9. Doctors
10. Psychiatrists
11. Registered nurses

12. Optometrists
13. Clinical psychologists

Available jobs unfilled represents money that is not circulating in the economy. To prepare a productive individual, the attempt must begin before conception. The Pittsburgh region continuously seeks qualified-skill individuals. We must "Train-Up a Child" for success, benefiting the self, family, nation, and world. It is never too early to begin preparing for a career in medicine. It is recommended that students take four years of math and four years of science in high school.

Undergraduate Degree

An undergraduate degree should include the following:

- Biology: Students satisfy by taking a one-year biology course, including lab that stresses molecular and quantitative concepts. Courses in anatomy, taxonomy, botany, and ecology will not satisfy this requirement but can supplement it.
- General chemistry through organic chemistry: To meet this requirement, the student must have completed a one-year course in basic chemistry with lab and a one-year course in organic chemistry lab.
- Basic physics: Students must take one-year course in physics with lab.
- Writing skills: Students must take one semester of an introductory course in expository writing.
- Biochemistry: A course in biochemistry is required.
- English and math should be taken early in college years.
- GPA of 3.7 is required to enter college premed.

Medical schools are looking for distinction in academic preparation, personal accomplishment, leadership, humanistic dedication, and passion for medicine research. Motivation, maturity, poise, integrity, inquisitive, perseverance, humility, responsibility to self and others, professionalism, and excellent communication skills are mandatory.

Youth Travel Education Experiences

Once a month on Saturday or Sunday or a weekday, the medical explorers are taken on a fun outing for development purposes. Just for Girls travels one day of the month. And Just for Boys travels on a different day of the month. Additional boys and additional girls travel with the medical explorer's boys and girls. You cannot offer high-quality education in the ghetto; therefore, they travel to locations to assist in developing social and psychological skills, such as the following:

- Pirates' baseball games
- University of Pittsburgh basketball game
- University of Pittsburgh football game
- middle and high school rodeo in North Washington, Pennsylvania
- *The Nutcracker* at the Benedum Center
- Two youth business meetings at Pittsburgh Athletic Association from 10:00 a.m. to 3:00 p.m. (bowling from 1:00–3:00 p.m.)
- "First Step: Mechanics of Starting a Small Business" at the University of Pittsburgh Institute for Entrepreneurial Excellence
- Carnegie Science Center
- Randall Industries in Cherry Tree, Pennsylvania (a chemical production company)
- The National Association of Black Engineers
- Romp 'n Roll roller skating
- Sesame Street LIVE-Elmo Makes Music
- Pittsburgh International Auto Show 2013

The medical explorers receive orientation on college life and SAT preparation from the University of Pittsburgh's medical students annually. Weekly students are given short reading assignments for SAT reading and vocabulary building. Also, they are encouraged to make good grades in school (As and Bs).

Entrepreneurial Training

In August 2014, And Step, Inc., vision traveling to the Freedom Foundation with twelve medical explorers (grades nine through eleven) for a six-day student entrepreneur experience. To qualify for this experience, all students must perform at least at the level of average or above average in the following abilities and characteristics.

- communication skills
- intellectual ability
- integrity
- personal motivation
- initiative
- ability to work independently
- responsibility/reliability
- leadership potential
- interpersonal skills
- quality of relationships
- emotional stability
- ability to handle stress
- service orientation
- sensitivity and empathy

Supervised by staff and faculty, each leadership team will be given the opportunity to create their own stock portfolios from descriptions of the members of the Dow Jones Industrial Average. Initially, they will be given a predetermined amount of investment financial capital. They then have seven days to generate the most capital (cash and equity) from their investments. The students calculate the new values of their portfolio on a daily basis. Market movement and outcomes that may result in subsequent changes in portfolio value will be distributed to the students at the beginning of each day.

Mandatory Travel Education

After completion of grade five, it is the vision that all students will have the following travel experiences.

- They will travel to Shirley Plantation in Virginia, which dates to 1616 when John Rolfe documented that Captain Isaac Madison oversaw twenty-five men planting and curing tobacco. These men were all white and indentured servants who were later replaced by slaves from Africa. On this same tour, students will visit Washington, DC, and also visit a beach for a day.
- They will take a two-night and three-day tour to New York City with beach time in New Jersey.
- They will experience a five-day Birth of a Free Nation visit at the Freedom Foundation (March or April).
- They will have a six-day Student Entrepreneur Experience at the Freedom Foundation (August).
- They will have a six-day Service Learning in Public Policy experience at the Freedom Foundation. A strong academic record (minimum 3.5 GPA) is required.

JUST FOR GIRLS

To prepare youth for these events, we must start at the cradle. Many young girls ages twelve, thirteen, and up already have had children. These girls, still children themselves, are in need of family holistic mentoring, including 24-7 childcare, parenting classes, one-on-one mentoring, family responsibilities, and appropriate living conditions.

Early Adolescence

Adolescence is a time of storm and stress, a period of upheaval, passion, and rebellion against authority. When children experience difficulty during adolescence, they will struggle with peer pressure, sexuality, or drug use. The age of puberty has declined by three years or more for many and as early as seven years old. Early maturation for males is advantageous because society places great value on athletic pursuits. Because they develop bulky muscles and have height, they tend to become popular leaders among their peers.

For the females, early maturation is not so advantageous. These girls look like young women even though they are still girls. They are faced with sexual innuendoes and pressure sooner than their peers and many become sexually active. As this author counsels females, some started their sexual encounters with adult males as early as age four. The cause is drugs (crack cocaine) and poverty. In 1995 when Rev. Baker wrote the And Step model, he received the following facts from Healthy Start, Inc

- Gonorrhea in 1992 was 1.6 percent in Allegheny County among teenagers.
- Nationally, the rate of gonorrhea was 0.8 percent.

- In the city of Pittsburgh, the rate was 3.6 percent, which is four times the national rate.

A child born in 1992 is now age twenty. If a mother has a sexually transmitted disease (STD) while she is pregnant, it could damage the unborn child in several ways, such as: heart disease, paralysis, blindness, deafness, insanity, and even death. Diseases like Chlamydia and gonorrhea, if undetected and untreated in girls and women, can lead to a painful condition known as pelvic inflammatory disease (PID) and cause permanent infertility. Drug use by one or both parents may also affect the fetus at conception. Crack cocaine use by the male is in the sperm that enters the egg. For the female, the drug enters the fetus through the placenta into umbilical cord.

If the teenage mother is not engaged and mentored, there is a great possibility that she will keep having babies. She needs love. The male offers love for sex, and the female offers sex for love. Both are short lived, and they both will most likely entertain several partners. The girl with child's lifeline is welfare. The male's lifeline is the neighborhood drug dealer. If you are selling drugs, it is absolutely essential to carry a weapon (gun). It is well understood by psychologists that serious adolescent problems tend to follow from serious childhood problems, which will most likely develop into antisocial personality disorder.

As written under pariah development, Sheila R. Staley states that many children from single-parent households experience their mother's rejection, anger, and frustration because they are constant reminders of her previous bad relationship with their father or of other troubled circumstances. As a result of their parents' rejection, the males seek comfort and solace in a gang *or in identification with a street man. Many young girls attempt to find acceptance and love in* an intimate relationship with a man. One must always keep in mind that it is the mother who raises the girl and teaches the boy love by respecting the father, and it is the father who raises the boy and teaches the girl respect by loving her mother. In other words, for both male and female, there is a deep need for love and acceptance, and if they do not find it, they will continue to search and drift.

All youth will experience an identity crisis. The task during the teen years is to establish a personal identity that is separate from their parents and peers. Going through the crisis, the youth question parents, peers, and all standards and norms. These hypothetical questions require formal operational thinking. After experiencing the crisis, in time one begins to establish a system of beliefs and choices. Those who have undergone the crisis and made resultant commitments will have achieved an identity. There are four identity states *(Baker Encyclopedia, 47-48)*.

1. *Identity diffusion* is the individuals who have neither experienced a crisis nor made a commitment. Most teens move beyond this level before completing high school.
2. *Moratorium* is the individuals who are currently in the state of crisis but who have not yet made commitments.
3. *Identity foreclosure* is individuals who have formed commitments without having experienced a crisis. They have accepted the values and choices of other people, usually parents and peers. This can be a dead end for some. For others it will eventually give way to a state of moratorium, leading to *identity achievement*.
4. *Negative identity and delinquency* is the individuals who go through a crisis and form commitments that are inconsistent with the values of society, such as the identity of a criminal.

Therefore, built into the "Train-Up a Child" nurturing/ mentoring model, Rev. Baker designed "Just for Girls." This holistic model is designed to nurture and mentor both boys and girls from the cradle to focus on handling the complexities of contemporary society, enhancing their self-confidence, motivation, and self-esteem. Both boys and girls also focus and practice character development, ethical decision making, formulating positive personal values, learning skills, social skills, and life skills.

STAFFING AND TRAINING

The staff is to be between the ages of eighteen and forty-five, with some post-high school education. Also, ex-military personnel (male and female) will be the most effective; they have the in-depth outdoor training that is necessary to give exposure. This age group sets the stage for present and future generations of children and youth. To be effective, understanding America's past negative behavior is relevant to effect positive change. You cannot understand where you are going unless you know from where you came. The public-school system nationwide does a very poor job of teaching these facts. Therefore, the following material resources will be used to enhance knowledge and understanding of self and the world in which we live.

- *Worse than Slavery* was written by David M. Oshinsky, professor of history at Rutgers University; it is a documentary of the Mississippi Delta black code set in motion after the emancipation of slaves. These codes are covertly active today nationwide.
- *The New Jim Crow* was written by Michelle Alexander; she is a civil rights advocate and litigator. Her documentary focuses on "Mass Incarceration in the Age of Colorblindness." By targeting black men through the War on Drugs and decimating communities of color, the US criminal justice system functions as a contemporary system of racial control.
- *The 7 Habits of Highly Effective Families is* written by Steven R. Covey. His principles about moving from survival, to stability, to success, to significance follow:

1. be proactive by becoming an agent of change.
2. Begin with the end in mind by developing a family mission statement.
3. Put first things first by making family a priority in a turbulent world.
4. Think win-win by moving from "me" to "we."
5. Seek first to understand ... then to be understood by solving family problems through empathic communication.
6. Synergize by building family unity through celebrating differences.
7. Sharpen the saw by renewing the family spirit through tradition.

- *Train up a Child* by R. B. Thieme (www.rbthieme.com) is a series of Bible doctrines written for teaching children an understanding of God. All children ask questions about God. Bad theology creates a void in the "soul" (self-awareness, mentality, conscious, and volition). This material is based on principles. Principles are universal, timeless, and self-evident. God is principle; He is the same yesterday, today, and forever.

STARTING A BUSINESS: ENTREPRENEURSHIP

(6) A Business Plan

                  (1) An Informed Entrepreneur

(5) An Ethics & Social
   Responsibility Plan

                  (2) The Right Product

(4) Specific Competitive Advantage

                  (3) The Right Market (Customers)

Entrepreneur: A person who creates and organizes a *new business*.

Nonprofit Business: A business that is *not* run for the purpose of making a profit but to increase the well-being of others in certain area, such as education, religion, health, and other causes.

Social Entrepreneur: A person who starts a business with a *social* issue as the primary focus.

Entrepreneurial Spirit: The fresh energy generated by needs and problems viewed as opportunities for innovation.

Product Development: Developing a new product or service or improving on an existing product or service.

Six Characteristics of Successful Entrepreneurs

1. **Perseveran**ce: Address challenges with determination and commitment to the *venture*.
2. **Innovative thinking**: This is the heart of starting, growing, and maintaining a successful entrepreneurial venture.
3. **elf-confidence**: This is the foundation of determination to pursue innovative ideas.
4. **Action-oriented**: Rapidly changing technology and high speed communication require trying several new things quickly.
5. **Communication/working with peo**ple: These are producers, suppliers, distributors, employees, customers, and business partners.
6. **Specific knowledge about the potential business venture:** If this is lacking, develop it as a priority—classes, internship, mentor, and/or get an entry-level position.

Demographic: A group sharing characteristics of a human population segments, used to identify consumer markets' wants and needs.

Marketing: The means by which a product or service is made known and sold to customers.

Competitive Advantage/Core business values: The expectation and behaviors of a business that set it apart from its competitors through improvements in quality, value, or delivery.

Ethic: The standards that help determine what is good, right, and proper. Ethics are what someone does when no one is looking.

Social Responsibility: A business's obligation to weigh the consequences to all stakeholders before making decisions.

Stakeholder: Any person or group directly affected by a business. This can include employees, suppliers, customers, community members, and shareholders.

The Six Business Structures

1. **Sole Proprietorship**: A sole proprietorship is the simplest and most common structure chosen to start a business. It is an unincorporated business owned and run by one individual with no distinction between the business and you, the owner. You are entitled to all profit and are responsible for all your business's debts, losses, and liabilities.

2. **Limited Liability Company:** A limited liability company is a hybrid type of legal structure that provides the limited liability features of a corporation and the tax efficiencies and operational flexibility of a partnership. The owners of an LLC are referred to as members. Depending on the state, the members can consist of a single individual (one owner), two or more individuals, corporations, or other LLCs. Unlike shareholders in a corporation, LLCs are not taxed as a separate business entity. Instead, all profits and losses are passed through the business to each member of the LLC. LLC members report profits and losses on their personal federal tax returns, just like the owners of a partnership would.

3. **Cooperative**: A cooperative is a business or organization owned by and operated for the benefit of those using its services. Profits and earnings generated by the cooperative are distributed among the members, also known as user owners. Typically, an elected board of directors and officers run the cooperative while regular members have voting power to control the direction of the cooperative. Members can become part of the cooperative by purchasing shares, though the amount of shares they hold does not affect the weight of their vote. Cooperatives are common in the health, retail, agriculture, art, and restaurant industries.

4. **Partnerships**: A partnership is the relationship existing between two or more persons who join to carry on a trade of business. Each person contributes money, property, labor or skill, and expects to share in the profits and losses of the business.

5. **Corporation (C Corporation)**: A corporation (sometimes referred to as a C corporation) is an independent legal entity owned by shareholders. This means that the corporation itself, not the shareholders that own it, is held legally liable for the actions and debts the business incurs.

6. **S Corporation**: An S corporation (sometimes referred to as an S corp.) is a special type of corporation created through an IRS tax election. An eligible domestic corporation can avoid double taxation (once to the corporation and again to the shareholders) by electing to be treated as an S corporation.

Franchise Business: A franchise is a business model that involves one business owner licensing trademarks and methods to an independent entrepreneur. Sometimes franchises are referred to as chains. There are two primary forms of franchising:

1. Product/trade name franchising: The franchisor owns the right to the name or trademark and sells that right to a franchise.

2. Business format franchising: The franchisor and franchisee have an ongoing relationship, and the franchisor often provides a full range of services, including site selection, training, product supply, marketing plans, and even assistance in obtaining financing.

To start a business, first register it in your state by completing the business structure forms and registration of a fictitious name. The website in Pennsylvania is www.paopenforbusines.state.pa.us or call (717) 987 1057. Next, apply for an EIN (employer identification number) by calling the IRS's Business and Specialty Tax line at (800) 829 4933

Note: Visit the following two websites for tutorials:

www.SBA.Gov (US Small Business Administration). Go "Learning Center."
www.IRS.Gov/Business

Business Plan

The following business plan is found in Judith B. Harrington's book *The Everything Start your own Business*, second edition, 288-98.

Goody Two-Shoes Cupcakes
"A little bit of heaven delivered in a cupcake."

Business Plan
Goody Two-Shoes Cupcakes Boston,
Massachusetts Phone: 617-883-1234
E-Mail: Cupcakes@bizland.com

Table of Contents

Executive Summary

Goody Two-Shoes Cupcakes will operate in a-store-front location selling cupcakes retail. It will also offer delivery of cupcakes on short notice, and will have a space to hold private functions such as birthday parties, teas, showers, or other themed celebrations. The retail location will be sited in the Boston/Brookline, Massachusetts area giving it access to an urban, suburban market accustomed to purchasing specialized food products. It will also be situated in an area saturated with college students who can order cupcakes delivered to their apartments or dormitories on short notice.

At present cupcakes can be purchased in bakeries and local grocery stores; however, there is no bakery outlet devoted exclusively to cupcakes. Nor do any purveyors (caterers) of cupcakes offer delivery.

Goody Two-Shoes Cupcakes will operate from 10 a.m. to 1 a.m. Monday to Saturday and noon to 9 p.m. on Sundays, with cupcakes being made throughout the day. During college exam periods deliveries will be available twenty-four hours a day. Staffing will consist of professional bakers working two shifts six days a week counter staff, delivery drivers, and a functions coordinator. Other business functions will be subcontracted.

One dozen flavors will be available every day with a rolling change of recipes and flavors. Home-style staples, such as devil's food with fudge icing and yellow cake with vanilla frosting, will always be available. Decorations will be themed to time of year, such as orange-iced chocolate cupcakes in October, pastel frosted in spring, etc. Both hot and cold beverages will be sold in the store and "boxes of Joe" can be ordered for deliveries. Accessories such as special towers to display cupcakes, candles, and related party paraphernalia will be offered in the store.

Start-up costs include outfitting a baker's kitchen with ovens, work tables, chillers, and pans and related equipment; the shop will require counter and display cases and small tables and chairs; a function room will need assorted tables and chairs. Shop and function room will be decoratively painted in whimsical fun style similar to old-fashioned ice-cream parlors. Patrons will be greeted with the aroma of cupcakes baking, upbeat music, friendly staff, and a clean, neat shop.

Marketing to professionals, homemakers, party planners, and college students will be done with promotions targeted to each.

Orders can be placed online or by telephone. Payment will be cash or credit card. We expect to add Goody Two-Shoes Cupcakes to college student pre-paid cards.

Industry Analysis

The Boston area is a market with one of the highest per capita incomes in the country. Many specialty markets, eateries, meat purveyors, fishmongers, and bakeries all survive because this is a market dominated by professionals and students who work long hours and do not have the time to prepare meals and dessert from scratch. Two Harvard Business School graduates have opened high-end dessert-only establishments in the theater district and Harvard Square, demonstrating interest in dessert-only offerings. At present no other cupcake-only bakery/cafes exist. The added feature of offering delivery on short notice will further differentiate this business.

By segmenting the business into three parts-in store retail, in-store private functions, and take-away orders-there is an opportunity to differentiate Goody Two-Shoes Cupcakes from other dessert sellers in the Boston area.

NOTE: This is where you would include relevant statistics that would support the likelihood for success of your venture, such as demographic growth of online purchases if you will be selling online, or trends in society, or the growth of demand for your product or service idea.

Business Overview

Goody Two-Shoes Cupcakes will initially be located in Chestnut Hill, area straddling Newton, Boston, and Brookline, Massachusetts. The retail store will be in a small strip mall with easy-access parking. In five years the goal is to have retail outlets in the downtown area of Boston, the South Shore, and Harvard Square. Each location will have a similar design, with an ice-cream parlor décor; however, the downtown location will only be retail with no function space.

A function space will be included in the South Shore location, but not deliveries. Deliveries will be from the main store in Chestnut Hill to greater Boston.

Only one central kitchen will be used to bake for all new locations, limiting expansion costs to retail space, staffing, and furnishings. A professional commercial kitchen designer will be used to plan the kitchen to make sure it meets all regulatory requirements. All inspections, registrations, handicap access compliance, etc. will be addressed in designing and outfitting bakery and shops.

Start-up expenses will include rental of space, interior design, outfitting with equipment and furnishings, insurance, licenses, deposits for supplies, utilities, advertising and promotion, Web site, and signs. Staffing will include one or two bakers on two shifts six days a week, counter sales staff, delivery drivers, and a function coordinator. When new branches are opened, only counter staff is needed. Professional services for back office functions of payroll and computer support will be subcontracted. General administration will be provided by Goody Two-Shoes Cupcakes business owner.

Products and Services

The primary product for Goody Two-Shoes Cupcakes will be cupcakes in various flavors and sizes. Varieties will vary seasonally and daily. Customers will be able to order cupcakes in three sizes: miniature, conventional, and oversize, which amounts to a traditional cake. An assortment of decorations will be available to choose from for custom orders.

Since the emphasis is on cupcakes as a dessert, the breakfast crowd will not be addressed. Operating hours will begin mid-morning for coffee breaks; or gathering products for desserts later in the day, and will end at 1 a.m. weekdays and 11:30 p.m. Friday and Saturday.

Drinks will be sold at the retail locations; hot coffee, tea, espresso, and hot chocolate and cold-water, milk, juice, and soft drinks. A beer and wine license will be secured for the primary location so that champagne, dessert wine, and beer can be offered with private functions.

Party accessories will be sold in the shops, including birthday and specialty candles, mugs, party hats, and platters, towers, and related items to display cupcakes at home. Custom orders can be made for take-away, or for an in house function. Nonalcoholic beverages can be ordered for takeaway orders, including a "box of Joe."

Besides offering a delicious and visually creative product, one of the distinguishing features of Goody

Two-Shoes Cupcakes will be the ability to phone in or e-mail an order to be delivered on short notice. With the saturated student market in greater Boston, delivery will be offered round the clock during exam periods.

Marketing Plan

Goody Two-Shoes Cupcakes will address four target audiences: busy professionals who may pick up the products to take home, or bring to the office; party planners; homemakers seeking a quick, non-fussy dessert for their family; and students seeking comfort food or something sweet to help get them through studies. Customers will have the option of buying cupcakes in the retail shop to eat in or take away, hosting a private party in the function space at the shop, or ordering cupcakes for delivery.

Web site will show daily cupcake flavors and special promotions. Advertisements will be placed in student newspapers, local papers, online yellow pages, local church bulletins, Boston magazine, Stuff@Nite, Improper Bostonian, parent publications, and regional wedding magazines.

Goody Two-Shoes Cupcakes is in negotiations with area colleges to be included in authorized off-campus outlet purchases on student cards. Private functions such as birthday parties for children, bridal showers, and ladies' teas will be promoted on the Web site and with direct-mail postcard promotions. School vacation tie-ins will be made with local movie theater.

A distinctive logo and colors will draw the attention of passersby seeing the sign and of readers of ads. Incentives such as a baker's dozen on Tuesdays, or a free cupcake for the birthday boy or girl, will be offered. A cupcake punch card will be used to keep customers coming back. A free cupcake will be earned after fifteen purchases.

For community service Goody Two-Shoes Cupcakes expects to support local school fairs and one or more charity walkathons. To entice the bridal market, Goody Two-Shoes will participate in local bridal shows, offering tastings. Special events will be offered at the store during slow times, such as the summer, to draw in customers.

Competitive Analysis

No other "cupcakes only" business exists currently in Boston area. Although cupcakes can be purchased at bakeries, coffee shops, grocery stores, and big box stores, no other outlet specializes in cupcakes. New York City has a number of cupcake stores, so the model does exist.

The three main business focus areas of Goody Two Shoes Cupcakes are: in-store sales, private functions in the store, and delivery on short notice. We are unaware of any bakeries that will deliver on short notice. We are also unaware of any bakeries or pastry shops offering a private function room. These two features, along with the specialized product – cupcakes – set Goody Two Shoes Cupcakes apart in a market awash in food outlets.

The challenge for Goody Two-Shoes Cupcakes will be to carve out its niche and remain the dominant player. Its goal is to offer a delicious, visually appealing product in a spotlessly clean, fun, welcoming environment. Customers having experienced Goody Two-Shoes Cupcakes will want to spread the word to their friends and come back again and again.

Customers will be asked to vote on their favorite flavors, and to challenge Goody Two-Shoes to replicate family recipes. In addition to making payments by check or credit card, students will be able to use their student cards to make purchases.

NOTE: If your business idea has you entering an established market such as coffee and espresso shops you will need to demonstrate how your idea will fill a niche.

Operations Plan

The bakery function will begin four hours before the store opens for business, and will continue throughout the day until four or five hours before closing, depending on how inventory is going. Sunday sales will be of product made on Saturday and refrigerated overnight.

Counter employees will arrive thirty minutes prior to opening to have store set and product displayed. A number dispenser will be employed to make sure customers are served in order. A plate of samples will be available at all times to promote increased sales.

Throughout the day, the floors will be swept and counters and tables will be wiped and kept clean; as will the bathrooms. Cleanliness will be an obsession. Store will be thoroughly cleaned at closing, with last employee leaving thirty to forty-five minutes after doors close.

Cash deposits will be made daily; cash-register tapes and credit-card charges will be reconciled each morning. Bakers will be responsible for keeping track of ingredient inventory, placing orders, and checking deliveries under supervision of store owners, who will handle orders for all other supplies and goods for retail sales.

Deliveries will be made by one staff driver and supplemented by taxi service in busy periods. A function coordinator will be responsible for selling and overseeing private parties in function room. The functions coordinator will represent Goody Two-Shoes Cupcakes at trade shows and bridal fairs to help sell private parties and special orders.

Payroll will be subcontracted to a payroll service, which will handle submitting withholding payments on behalf of business, issuing W-2s, 1099s, and other relevant filings. A part-time bookkeeper will be employed to handle payable and any private function receivables. Regular reports will be generated to track sales, popular flavors, cash flow, variables in overhead expenses, etc. Peak times will be monitored so staffing levels can be adjusted.

Management Team Elizabeth and John Richardson are the founders of Goody Two-Shoes Cupcakes. John, a graduate of the Culinary Institute of America, has been head baker and pastry chef for a local chain of gourmet to-go food shops in the Boston area for the past ten years. Previous to studying at the CIA he was a student at the Museum School in Boston and had a part-time job as a delivery driver for restaurants in the Cleveland Circle area. Elizabeth, a graduate of the Hotel School at Cornell University, was the function manager for several years at the ABC Fancy restaurant in Harvard Square, where she most recently has been the business manager. Their combined professional experience, training and undying interest in making simple things special have led them to this business concept.

Five Major Steps in Funding a Business Venture

Step 1: Start-up cost

Step 2: Monthly expenses

Step 3: Cash-flow statement--actual cash flow needs to be compared to projected cash-flow on a monthly basis.

Step 4: Other financial statements: The break-even point

A. The Income Statement: Total income and total expenses

B. Balance Sheet: A snapshot of assets and liabilities of the business
   1. Assets: Things owned by the business
   2. Liabilities: Obligations of the business

C. Net Worth: The equity of the business

Note: Financial states the to-do list and summary

1. *Make a list of all start-up costs.*
2. *Estimate your fixed and variable monthly expenses.*
3. *Start to prepare your cash-flow statement.*

Step 5: Financing your business (many businesses fail because of inadequate capital)

A. Sources of financing: personal savings, partner, friends and relatives, and banks and credit unions

B. The five C's of credit the bank must consider

1. Capacity to repay
2. Capital—money you are personally investing
3. Collateral—a second source of repayment
4. Conditions—intended purpose of the loan: work capital, additional equipment, or inventory. Also, what is the local economic climate within the industry and other areas?
5. Character—lender's subjective opinion of sufficiently trustworthiness.

Loan-Packaging Requirements: Business plan with financial plans and projection

TWENTY-FIRST CENTURIES HOLISTIC FAMILY LIFE DEPARTMENTS

It is the vision of the author that a Twenty-First Century Holistic Family Life Institution is essential in the East-End, which will accommodate the following departments:

- a twenty-four-hour certified child development center, including door-to-door pickup and drop-off
- regenerative medicine (biotechnology and bioengineering) programs for kindergarten to twelfth grade, including door to-door pickup and drop-off
- Head Start for ages three and four
- parent education from infancy up
- Driver education/driver and training/transportation
- twenty-four-hour auto repair
- vehicle insurance
- property acquisition, management, repairs
- property insurance and taxes
- financial accounting, banking, payroll
- life insurance and investments
- estate planning/endowment
- crises intervention/grief and grief recovery
- workforce development (job placement and mentoring)

Character, leadership, and entrepreneurial principles are ubiquitous.

ESTATE PLANNING

Estate planning encompasses the accumulation, conservation, preservation, and transfer of an estate through planning and implementation of an estate plan. The overall purpose of the estate planning process is to develop a plan that will maintain the financial security of individuals and their families. Estate planning has come to include and mean lifetime planning that leads to creation, conservation, and transfer of assets. Estate planning should also facilitate the intended and orderly transfer of property at death, taking into consideration the family unit and the potential costs of different methods. Estate-planning activities could include the following functions appropriate to the applicant's respective discipline(s):

- administering estates and trusts
- analyzing existing life insurance coverage for continuing relevance
- analyzing proposed transactions for estate and gift tax implications
- attending estate-planning council meetings and other estate planning educational events
- business succession planning
- charitable/gifting planning
- designing estate plans
- designing qualified and nonqualified retirement plans
- developing strategies to minimize potential estate and gift taxes
- developing programs to conserve assets during lifetime and at death

- drafting estate-planning documents
- life settlement of life insurance policies
- preparing estate and gift tax returns
- preparing fiduciary accountings
- preparing fiduciary income tax returns
- probating wills and administering estates
- proposing life insurance solutions consistent with estate plans
- retirement distribution planning
- succession planning
- estate, gifts, and/or generation-skipping taxes

One of the main financial problems of African Americans is the lack of a family financial legacy. Every generation has to start without any insight of the future

BANKING EDUCATION

The at-risk have very little knowledge in banking. The inner-city school districts do not focus on financial literacy. The Dollar Bank uses the following banking education program. The program consists of training modules that can be used independently of each other. Based on the objectives of the instructor and the amount of time allotted, modules can be condensed or expanded. The information can be delivered in one day or presented over the course of several sessions

Middle School Students Grades Five through Eight

- Checking Module The checking module shows students how to use a checking account responsibly. The module allows students to practice writing checks and using deposit and withdrawal slips.
- The Basics of a Checking Account (thirty to forty minutes)
  What is a checking account?
  How can a checking account help you?
  What does the bank require you to have to open an account?
  What other bank services can you use with a checking account?

- Managing a Checking Account (thirty to forty minutes)
  How to access money in a checking account Ways to make a deposit into an account Ways to make a withdrawal from an account The proper way to write a check . Check writing practice exercise

- Group Activities
  Completing deposit and withdrawal slips Check writing practice exercise Recording information in a check register Balancing a check register

- Savings Module
- The savings module helps students identify ways they can save money and introduces them to the options they have for saving money. It emphasizes the importance of saving money for goals and future needs.
- Pay Yourself First (ten minutes)
  Pay yourself first means making it a priority to save
  What are the benefits of paying yourself first?
  What are some of the ways you can begin to save right now?
- How Your Money Can Grow (fifteen minutes)
  What is interest?
  What does compound interest mean?
  Using an interest calculator to determine how much you can earn

- Saving Options (fifteen minutes)
  Banking savings account products such as passbooks, statement savings, certificates of deposit
  Investment account options such as stocks, bonds, mutual funds
  Creating a Savings Plan (fifteen minutes)
  Students will work on an action plan for saving Money
  Students will discuss ways to increase the amount they save

- **Credit Module**

The credit module helps students understand what credit is and how it works. It also discusses the importance of using credit responsibly and wisely. *This module may not be applicable to all middle school students. Therefore, it will be important for you to know their level of understanding.*

- Understanding Credit (twenty-five minutes)
    What is credit?
    Why is credit important?
    Why do people take out loans?
    The types of loans are available
    The costs associated with having credit

- Understanding a Credit Report (fifteen minutes)
    What is a credit report?
    The information contained in a credit report
    How credit reports are used

- Using Credit Cards (thirty minutes)
    The purpose of credit cards
    Types of credit cards
    What happens if a credit card is lost or stolen?
    Making payments; what happens if you make only the
        minimum payment?
    Ways to avoid the credit card trap
    The importance of using a credit card wisely

For Grades Eight to Twelve

How credit card companies determine approvals and credit limits
Credit card terminology; APR, fees, grace period, balance transfers,
balance computation methods, etc. Application requirements

- Budgeting Module
    The budgeting module teaches students the importance
        of managing their money and introduces them to
        the concept of creating a budget.

- The Essentials of Budgeting (fifteen minutes)
  What is a budget?
  How can a budget help you manage your money?
  What are the advantages of creating a budget?

- Understanding Income and Expenses (fifteen minutes)
  What is income?
  How can we increase our income?
  What is an expense?
  What is the difference between fixed expenses and flexible expenses?
  How can we decrease expenses?

- The Steps to Creating an Effective Budget (twenty minutes)
  Keep track of daily spending
  Determine your monthly expenses and income
  Find ways to modify your spending
  Students will work on a daily budget track worksheet to help them figure out how much they spend in a typical day

- Understanding Wants and Needs (fifteen minutes)
  Needs are things we must have to survive
  Wants are things we would like to have but can do without
  Students will discuss the difference between wants and needs
  Using a budget will help you save for wants

- Group Activity (twenty minutes)
  Students will complete a budget planning worksheet to show them how to begin the process of creating a budget
  The group will discuss ways they can manage their money more effectively

For Grades Eight to Twelve

- Identity Theft Module
  The identity theft module explains the crime of identity theft. It outlines what identity theft is and why it is the fastest-growing crime in the United States. The module also reviews ways students can protect themselves against this crime

- Understanding Identity Theft (fifteen minutes)
  What is identity theft?
  What is fraud?
  Identity theft facts and statistics; how many people become victims each year, why teens can be targets

- Stealing Personal Information (fifteen minutes)
  How do thieves get someone's personal information?
  Thieves use personal information to open bank accounts, establish credit cards, write bad checks, create false identification, etc.

- Protecting yourself from identity theft (fifteen minutes)
  Students will discuss the things they can do to keep their personal information safe

XYZ EMPLOYMENT APPLICATION

Some positions may require completion of a multiple choice, typing, or other job-related test. *Please indicate if you need accommodation to complete the application process* __YES__NO

Personal Information

Name (Last, First, Middle)

Male____   Female____   Age____

Street Address   City   State   Zip

Telephone no. where you can be contacted

Have you ever worked XYZ?__Yes __No
If Yes, where and when?

Date First Employment
(if former employee)

Have you ever been convicted of a criminal offense within the past seven years (except minor traffic offenses)? If yes, give details.
__Yes _No

Can you upon employment, submit verification of your legal right to work in the United States and documentation verifying your identity? Referred by:

EMPLOYMENT INTEREST

Position for which you are applying: Salary Expected

Date Available   ____ full-time ____ Part-time

With regard to initial work location, do you have any geographic preferences? __Yes__No
If yes, specify

Are you willing to travel? __ Yes __ No
If yes, what percent?

Are there any hours, shifts, or days you cannot Or will not work?
__Yes__No
If yes, explain.

STORE POSITIONS ONLY: Please indicate the days and hours you are available to work. Be sure to state AM or PM.

MONDAY: WEDNESDAY: FRIDAY:
TUESDAY: THURSDAY: SATURDAY:
SUNDAY:

Certain positions within the company may require use of a car or other motorized vehicle. If you use such a vehicle where required in the job for which you are applying ...

A. So you have a valid driver's license? __Yes__No
B. Do you have access to a car or other motorized vehicle?
__Yes__No
C. Do you have or can you get liability insurance on such a vehicle?
__Yes__No

Your driving record will be checked if you drive a company vehicle.

Other specialized skills or information you feel are pertinent to the job for which you are applying

Education

Highest Grade,   Course/Major
Diploma Or Degree   High School College

Business,
Vocational
   or
Other Training

Employment History Information Will Be Verified; Telephone Numbers Are Very Important

Please list *all jobs,* beginning with your present or last employer. Account for all time periods, including *Unemployment, Self-Employment,* and U.S. *Military Service.* If space is insufficient, list on a separate page or additional application form.

1. Name and Address   Dates of Employment   Salary
   Start   End   Start   End

Job Title   Department   Supervisor
May we contact your employer? __Yes _No   Telephone. Num.

Type of Business   Duties and Responsibility
Reason for leaving

2. Name and Address   Dates of Employment   Salary
   Start   End   Start   End

Job Title   Department   Supervisor
May we contact your employer? __Yes _No   Telephone. Num.

Type of Business   Duties and Responsibility
Reason for leaving

3. Name and address   Dates of Employment   Salary
   Start   End   Start   End

Job Title   Department   Supervisor
May we contact your employer? __Yes _No   Telephone. Num.

Type of Business   Duties and Responsibility
Reason for leaving

This company XYZ is committed to programs of equal employment, which include giving full consideration to qualifications for employment of applicants who: a) have a physical or mental health conditions that may be regarded as a disability; b) are disabled veterans; or c) are veterans of the Vietnam era. You may volunteer this information to the employment representation when you submit this application. You may also provide information on the skills and/or procedures you use or intend to use to perform the job for which you are applying and the nature and type of accommodations you feel an employer may need to make to enable you to perform the job in a proper and safe manner. This information will be treated as confidential. Failure to provide information will not jeopardize or adversely affect any consideration you may receive for employment.

I certify the facts set forth in my application for employment are true and complete. I understand that, if employed, false statements in this application may be considered sufficient cause for dismissal. I authorize XYZ to verify all statements contained in this application and to contact schools, former employers, and to investigate my personal and my professional background necessary and as limited above for my present employer. I authorize and release any and all former and/or present employers from liability whatsoever in connection with XYZ's attempts to verify my past employment. I also understand that, if employed I will be required to complete the Immigration Service form 1-9 for employment eligibility and show required supporting documentation.

I hereby authorize and direct the employer to withhold and deduct from my paycheck or from any monies owed me or held for me said employer all or any portion thereof upon the amount of, and in payment of, any indebtedness I may have said employer at time of termination of employment.

Applicant's Signature_____   Date

TRAVEL VEHICLES

In the ghetto, transportation is a major issue. Parents do not have vehicles to drop off and pick up their children from an educational center. The majority do not have a driver's licenses. Also, those who have a driver's license have very minimal vehicle maintenance knowledge. "An ounce of prevention is worth a pound of cure." Routine auto maintenance can prevent a lot of costly problems, some of which could damage the vehicle and even endanger the driver and passengers. By properly maintaining a vehicle, one can spot problems as they develop and extend the vehicle's life by several years.

For any organization to be effective in the "Train-Up a Child" nurturing/mentoring model, it must purchase fifteen-passenger vans. The twelve-passenger vans are a waste of money. A minimum of three fifteen-passenger E-350 Ford vans for door-to-door pickup and travel education are essential. For And Step, Inc.'s effectiveness, three smaller vehicles (all-wheel-drive SUVs) are needed for driver training for both parents/adults and youth. All staff must obtain driver's licenses and become skillful drivers.

School to Work

Every child lives sheltered in a building. Buildings need repairs from time to time. Teaching basic home repairs will give youth a sense of personal pride in their achievements; it will also increase self-confidence and enable the youth to save thousands of dollars in repair bills over the years. It is And Step, Inc.'s intention to obtain the abandoned and blighted properties and use them to train youth in entrepreneurship. Hopefully some choose this as a discipline for a career. The repairs to these homes are training grounds for the at risk (ages sixteen up, including young adults under age thirty-seven) school to work, which is built into the Workforce Development Institution. There are many skilled trades to be introduced, such as the following:

- electrician
- building engineering
- plumber/pipe-fitting
- painting occupations
- carpenter/woodworking
- building contractor
- Model design and building.

> Note: This is a combination of architecture and engineering. Architecture is the art of designing buildings. Architects and engineers often use models to see how the buildings they design will look, in miniature, before construction begins on the full-scale structure. The principles, including personal safety, the youth (grade four and up) learn are lifelong, They learn the use of the model-maker's hand tools, such as: knives, handsaws, vises, files, hammers, screwdrivers, hand drills and bits, pliers, and portable power tools. They also learn to build to scale, which uses math. The principles of architecture and engineering are used in many model designs, such as aircrafts, submarines, cars, trains, boats, houses, and more.

- flooring
- architecture and landscape architecture
- appliance repair
- heavy equipment operator
- surveyor

These are learning experiences through exposure and practice. Learning at its best occurs when individuals discover from within the facts and feelings about themselves and their world where they experience the integration of cognitive (knowledge) awareness with affective (feeling) awareness.

Twenty-Four-Hour Certified Automotive Service

The twenty-four-hour certified automotive mechanic service mentees are exposed to and practice automotive mechanic and automotive body repair.

- Many mentees' parents have been convicted of felonies.
- There are several opportunities for their training and development
- Student ages twelve to fifteen will be introduced to and practice entrepreneurship.
- At the age of fourteen, they will attend the six-day Student Entrepreneurial Experience.
- As a business owner, And Step, Inc., will contract appropriate projects to them, such as: car washing, lawn work, minor home repairs, equipment repairs, and cleanups.
- Many will also work in administrative areas.
- All students ages twelve to fifteen will receive stipends.
- Those age sixteen and up will receive wages.
- Student ages fifteen will attend driver education training in And Step, Inc.'s driving school
- At the age of sixteen, youth are to obtain a driver's license.
- At the age of eighteen, youth are to obtain commercial driver's licenses (CDL).

CHARACTER, LEADERSHIP, AND ENTREPRENEURIAL TRAINING

Material Resources

- Several material resources will be used to teach character, leadership, and entrepreneurial principles:
- *The 7 Habits of Highly Effective Teens* is written by Sean Covey. It will be used in group discussions to engage teenagers to address tough issues and life-changing decisions they face.

  1. Be Proactive: I am the force.
  2. Begin with the End in Mind: Control your own destiny or someone else will.
  3. Put First Things First: There is will and won't power.
  4. Think Win-Win: Life is an all-you-can-eat buffet.
  5. Seek First to Understand, Then to Be Understood: You have two ears and one mouth.
  6. Synergize: Take the "highway".
  7. Sharpen the Saw: It's me time.

- *Principle-Centered Leadership* is written by Stephen R. Covey. This book addresses the eight characteristics of principle-centered leaders:

  1. They are continually learning.
  2. They are service-oriented.
  3. They radiate positive energy.

4. They believe in other people.
5. They lead balanced lives.
6. They see life as an adventure.
7. They are synergistic.
8. They exercise for self-renewal.

*   *Series 6 License Exam Manual* is written by Kaplan Financial. It thoroughly addresses investment company products/ variable contracts in six units:

1. Securities Markets, Investment Securities, and Economic Factors
2. Product Information: Investment Company Securities and Variable Contracts
3. Securities and Tax Regulations
4. Marketing, Prospecting, and Sales Presentations
5. Evaluation of Customers
6. Opening and Servicing Customer Accounts

BUILDING ENGINEER WORKFORCE INVESTMENT DEPARTMENT

By understanding the job description of a building engineer, training may begin at home by the parent.

Building Engineer Job Description:

Taking responsibility for the daily operation of: maintenance, preventative maintenance, and repairs to a downtown thirty-five unit condominium complex plumbing, electrical, HVAC, and all other building systems. Must have working knowledge of all building mechanical, electrical, HVAC, plumbing, life safety, fire protection, and security systems to ensure proper operations and be able to act upon any conditions that are out of the ordinary.

Essential Job Duties

1. Inspect buildings, grounds, and equipment for unsafe or malfunctions.
2. Conduct periodic general preventative maintenance on the mechanical, electrical, HVAC, and plumbing system. This involves normal lubrication, adjustment, cleaning, replacement of consumable parts (such as filters, indicator lights, etc.), and periodic testing of the equipment. These systems include but are not limited to: air-handling units (including both rooftop and built-in units), re-circulating air systems, water-pumping systems, cooling plants, and all plumbing systems.

3. Assist with installation and modification of building equipment systems
4. Respond quickly to emergency situations.
5. Perform and/or oversee electrical and plumbing repair and troubleshooting.
6. Perform and/or oversee water treatment and testing.
7. Perform all assigned work to ensure the safety of the building's tenants and the continuous operation of the site.
8. Prioritize service calls and follow up upon completion.
9. Troubleshoot, evaluate, and recommend equipment/service upgrades.
10. Coordinate maintenance efforts with outside contractors and technicians when work cannot be performed in-house. Coordinate contractors, tenant and management approvals for work orders that require the use of an outside contractor. Maintain log of work order details.
11. Order parts and supplies as required, and maintain stock and inventory control.
12. Work with building manager in planning and controlling annual and capital budgets.
13. Be responsive to tenant complaints in the areas of safety, plumbing, mechanical, electrical, and environmental needs through both personal contact and work order systems.
14. Prepare and maintain maintenance logs and records.
15. Be familiar with and conform to all written operating procedures associated with site.
16. Ensure the cleanliness and appearance of all work areas.
17. Perform other duties as assigned.

Skills, Education, and Experience

- bachelor's degree or equivalent combination of education and experience
- minimum of five years of experience in building operation, engineering, and equipment and systems maintenance
- ability to handle multiple projects and make decisions

- holds necessary/required licenses
- completion of college or technical school HVAC certificates upon completions
- have knowledge and understanding of blueprints
- completion of building operator program coursework, engineering technical training, building operations and maintenance training certificates of completion
- possession of driver's license
- strong customer service, communication, and computer skills

Other Job Requirements

- available and on call 24-7
- have a personal van/truck
- able to lift fifty pounds
- able to climb ladder

Please send your resume and three references to:

Property Ownership

Property ownership is And Step, Inc.'s means of becoming equitable, and sustainable while creating a desirable community on the continuum of the East-End communities and Allegheny County. Assuming eight hundred green properties would average five hundred dollars a month, the gross income would be $4,800,000 a year in the Wilkinsburg Borough. The profit will be used for educational travel, for family support, and to endow the Twenty-First Century Holistic Family Life Institution.

SECTION 6

BECOMING AN
AMERICAN CITIZEN
(DEVELOPED CHARACTER, LEADERSHIP,
AND ENTREPRENEURIAL PRINCIPLES)

THE HISTORY OF THE BAKERS OF GATES COUNTY, NORTH CAROLINA

Gates County Census Records

Now we will examine my roots and my beginning, for unless you know where you came from, you can lose sight of where you are going. This historical and genealogical research from Gates County Census Records was completed by Roger W. Baker's first cousin, Moses A. Hardy Jr., who is the author of In *the Shadow of Kings*.

The original name of our ancestors was not Baker. None of the families on the West Coast of Africa were named Baker. Our current name was given to us by the slave owners who owned us prior to the abolishment of slavery. People from West Africa, at the time of slavery, did not look like me complexion-wise. In many instances, black women were forced to have children with white slave owners. The child that was produced was a fair-complexioned child called a mulatto (one parent was white (male) and one was black (female]).

Blake Baker Sr.

The 1850 census records for the state of North Carolina, County of Gates, enumerated on August 28, the assistant marshal listed the names and families of Blake Baker Sr. and his sons, Blake Baker Jr. and Marmaduke Baker. Blake Sr. was seventy-seven years old (born in 1778), and his occupation was "farmer." His real estate property was valued at $912 (a substantial amount of property in 1850).

Living in his household were the following:

- Bracy, age twenty-nine
- Emiline, age five
- Nancy, age fifty-six
- Perry, age twenty-nine
- Mary, age twenty-six
- Riddick, age three
- William, age one

Last Will and Testament

In 1855, Blake Baker Sr. wrote his last will and testament. In his will he gave land, property, and slaves to his children and grandchildren. The wording in the will was as follows: "I give & bequeath to my son Samuel Baker, one Negro girl Venus, one boy Peter & one boy Jordan, them & their increase to him & his heirs forever." He also gave to his son John a Negro girl named Hannah. In the minds of white people, slavery was forever. They had no idea that it would end.

The Civil War was about the abolishment of slavery.

In 1860 another census was recorded, and Marmaduke had fourteen slaves. The five mentioned earlier in the 1850 census were still a part of the Baker plantation. The ages are not exactly accurate; there were no birth certificates or family records.

- Nancy was now sixty-five.
- Mary was thirty-six.
- Riddick was eleven.
- William was ten.
- A new child had been born since the last census, James,
- who was six.
- Marmaduke's daughter, Margaret Humphlett, was
- twenty-nine.
- His granddaughter, Henrietta Humphlett, was ten.
- His brother, Samuel Baker, was sixty-five.
- Blake Jr., who lived on property adjacent to his father,

- Marmaduke, was thirty-one.
- His wife, Mary, was twenty-one.
- Five other family members were listed.

You will note that the slave named Perry was missing. It is thought that he was living on the farm of one of the other Baker brothers.

Marmaduke Baker

An older son, Marmaduke Baker, a farmer, age forty-nine, is the topic of much of this focus. The earliest traceable roots of the family begin with him. Marmaduke's real estate property was valued at twelve hundred dollars. Listed in his household are the following:

- his wife, Sarah, age thirty-eight
- a son, James, age twenty-one
- a daughter-in-law, Sarah E., age nineteen
- wife of Richard Baker, whereabouts unknown
- a daughter, Martha, age thirteen
- sons Joseph, Solomon, and Marmaduke Jr., ages thirteen, eight, and seven
- A daughter, Collette, age two

Blake Baker Sr. also had the following sons and daughters.

- Levi Baker
- John Baker
- Elizabeth Baker
- Denton James B. Baker

You may already begin to notice some familiar names, such as John, James, and Sarah.

Most blacks were slaves prior to 1864. In 1850, Marmaduke Baker owned ten slaves, and old man Blake owned thirteen. The slaves were listed on a schedule that listed the name of the owner, the number, ages, sex, and color of their slaves. They were not listed by name; therefore, the only way to trace heritage is to match ages and sex. Five of Marmaduke slaves stand out because of their age and sex, which are tied together later in this writing.

The first official record of black Bakers appears in 1870, six years after the Emancipation Proclamation. Perry Baker (the first one) was now fifty-one years old, which would make his year of birth 1819. Perry's wife, Mary, was now forty-five years old. Four children are listed.

- Riddick, age twenty-three
- William, age nineteen
- James, age sixteen
- Joseph, age one

Also living in the household was a Lucy Copeland, age seven. Living in an adjacent house was Nancy Baker, age seventy.

If Nancy was the slave identified in 1850 and 1860, her correct age should be seventy-five or seventy-six. Depending upon which record is correct, her birth year would have been between 1796 and 1800. It is believed that Nancy was the mother of Perry, making her our oldest known ancestor. It is very likely that some or all of Nancy's children were fathered by a white male in the Baker's Klan. According to this census, none of the family members could read or write. We do not know if this was true, but it was not popular for blacks to be able to read.

Riddick Baker

In 1880, the Gatesville Township Census shows a family headed by Riddick Baker, age thirty-three, and his wife, Hannah, age thirty. Hannah is believed to be the same "Negro girl" given to John Baker by his dying father in 1855. Two children are listed:

- a son, James Anthony, age three
- a daughter, Texana, age one

Most of the 1890 census records were destroyed by fire. The census of 1900 lists Riddick, age fifty-three, and his date of birth as May 1847. Hannah was age fifty, with a birth date January 1850. It also indicates that she was the mother of twelve children. Only four were presently living. James and Texana were still living at home. A son, Perry, now age nineteen, and a son, Hillory, age seventeen, had been born since the 1880 census.

Perry Baker was Roger W. Baker's grandfather and the father of the following people:

- Arthur Baker
- Gennette Baker
- John Baker, the father of the author, Roger W. Baker
- James Baker
- Sarah Baker, the mother of the researcher of this document, Moses A. Hardie Jr.
- Clementine Baker
- Mamie Baker

This is the unofficial history of the Bakers of Gates County. Research was completed July 1996 by Moses A. Hardie Jr.

HISTORIC DOCUMENT (BILL OF RIGHTS AND LATER AMENDMENTS)

Bill of Rights

Amendment 1: Freedoms, Petitions,

Amendment 2: Rights to Bear Arms

Amendment 3: Quartering of Soldiers

Amendment 4: Search and Arrest

Amendment 5: Rights in Criminal Cases

Amendment 6: Right to Fair Trial

Amendment 7: Rights in Civil Cases

Amendment 8: Bail, Fines,

Amendment 9: Rights Retained by the People

Amendment 10: States' Rights

Later Amendments

Amendment 11: Lawsuits against

Assembly States

Amendment 12: Presidential Elections

Amendment 13: Abolition of Slavery

Amendment 14: Civil Rights

Amendment 15: Black Suffrage

Amendment 16: Income Taxes

Amendment 17: Senatorial Elections

Amendment 18: Prohibition of Punishment Liquor

Amendment 19: Women's Suffrage

Amendment 20: Terms of Office

Amendment 21: Repeal of Prohibition

Amendment 22: Terms of Office

Amendment 23: Washington, DC, Suffrage

Amendment 24: Abolition of Poll Taxes

Amendment 25: Terms Limited for the Presidency

Amendment 26: Eighteen-Year-Old Suffrage

Amendment 27: Congressional Pay Raises

The original ten amendments, the Bill of Rights, was passed by Congress on September 25, 1789, and ratified December 15, 1791 (www.ushistory.org).

Amendment I
Freedoms, Petitions, Assembly

Congress shall make no law respecting an establishment of religion, or prohibiting the free exercise thereof; or abridging the freedom of speech, or of the press, or the right of the people peaceably to assemble, and to petition the Government for a redress of grievances.

Amendment II
Right to Bear Arms

A well regulated Militia, being necessary to the security of a Free State, the right of the people to keep and bear Arms, shall not be infringed.

Amendment III
Quartering of Soldiers

No Soldier shall, in time of peace be quartered in any house without the consent of the Owner, nor in time of war, but in a manner to be prescribed by law.

Amendment IV
Search and Arrest

The right of the people to be secure in their persons, houses, papers, and effects, against unreasonable searches and seizures, shall not be violated, and no Warrants shall issue, but upon probable cause, supported by Oath or affirmation, and particularly describing the place to be searched, and the persons or things to be seized.

Amendment V
Rights in Criminal Cases

No person shall be held to answer for a capital, or otherwise infamous crime, unless on a presentment or indictment of a Grand Jury, except in cases arising in the land or naval forces, or in the Militia, when in actual service in time of War or public danger; nor shall any person be subject for the same offence to be twice put in jeopardy of life or limb, nor shall be compelled in any criminal case to be a witness against himself, nor be deprived of life, liberty, or property, without due process of law; nor shall private property be taken for public use, without just compensation.

Amendment VI
Rights to a Fair Trial

In all criminal prosecutions, the accused shall enjoy the right to a speedy and public trial, by an impartial jury of the State and district wherein the crime shall have been committed; which district shall have been previously ascertained by law, and to be confronted with the witnesses against him; to have compulsory process for obtaining witnesses in his favor, and to have the assistance of counsel for his defense.

Amendment VII
Rights in Civil Cases

In Suits at common law, where the value in controversy shall exceed twenty dollars, the right of trial by jury shall be preserved, and no fact tried by a jury shall be otherwise re-examined in any Court of the United States, than according to the rules of the common law.

Amendment VIII
Bail, Fines, Punishment
Excessive bail shall not be required, nor excessive fines imposed, nor cruel and unusual punishment inflicted.

Amendment IX
Rights Retained by the People
The enumeration in the Constitution of certain rights shall not be construed to deny or disparage others retained by the people.

Amendment X
States' Rights
The power not delegated to the United States by the Constitution, nor prohibited by it to the States are reserved to the States respectively, or to the people.

Later Amendments

Amendment 11
Lawsuits against States
The Judicial power of the United States shall not be construed to extend to any suit in law or equity, commenced or prosecuted against one of the United States by Citizens of another State, or by Citizens or Subjects of any Foreign States.

Amendment 12
Presidential Elections
The Electors shall meet in their respective states, and vote by ballot for President and Vice-President, one of whom, at least, shall not be an inhabitant of the same state with themselves; they shall name in their ballots the person voted for as President, and in distinct ballots the person voted for as Vice-President, and they shall make distinct list of all persons voted for as President, and of all persons voted for as Vice-President, and of the number of votes for each, which list they shall sign and certify, and transmit sealed to the seat of the government of the United States, directed

to the President of the Senate;--The President of the Senate shall, in the presence of Senate and House of Representatives, open all the certificates and the votes shall then be counted;--The person having the greatest number of votes for President, shall be the President, if such number bed a majority of the whole number of Electors appointed; and if no person have such majority, then from the person having the highest numbers not exceeding three on the list of those voted for as President, the House of Representatives shall choose immediately, by ballot, the President. But in choosing the President, the votes shall be taken by states, the representation from each state having one vote; a quorum for this purpose shall consist of a member or members from two-thirds of the states and a majority of all the states shall be necessary to a choice. [And if the House of Representative shall not choose a President whenever the right of choice shall devolve upon them, before the fourth day of March next following, then the Vice-President shall act as President, as in the case of the death or other constitutional disability of the President.]* The person having the greatest number of votes as Vice-President, shall be the Vice President, if such number be a majority of the whole number of Electors appointed, and if no person have a majority, then from the two highest numbers on the list, the Senate shall choose the Vice President; a quorum for the purpose shall consist of two-thirds of the whole numbers of Senators, and a majority of the whole number shall be necessary to a choice. But no person constitutionally ineligible to the office of President shall be eligible to that of Vice-President of the United States.

June 15, 1804.
Superseded by Section 3 of the Twentieth Amendment.

Amendment 13
Abolition of Slavery

Section 1. Neither slavery nor involuntary-servitude, except as a punishment for crime whereof the party shall have been duly convicted, shall exist within the United States or any place subject to their jurisdiction.

Section 2. Congress shall have power to enforce this article by appropriate legislation.

December 6, 1865

Amendment 14
Civil Rights

Section 1. All persons born or naturalized in the United States and subject to the jurisdiction thereof are citizens of the United States and of the State wherein they reside. No State shall make or enforce any law which shall abridge the privilege or immunities of citizens of the United States; nor shall any State deprive any person of life, liberty, or property, without due process of law; nor deny to any person within its jurisdiction the equal protection of the laws.

Section 2. Representatives shall be apportioned among the several States according to their respective numbers, counting the whole number of persons in each State, excluding Indians not taxed. But when the right to vote at any election for the choice of electors for President and Vice-President of the United States, Representative in Congress, the Executive and Judicial officers of a State, or the members of the Legislature thereof, is denied to any of the male inhabitants of such State, being twenty-one years of age, and citizen of the United States, or in any abridged, except for participation in rebellion, or other crime, the basis of representation therein shall be reduced in the proportion which the number of such male citizens shall bear to the whole number of male citizens twenty-one years of age in such State.

Section 3. No person shall be a Senator or Representative in Congress, or elector of President and Vice-President, or hold any office, civil or military, under the United States, or under any State, who, having previously taken an oath, as a member of Congress, or as an officer of the United States, or as a member of any State legislature, or as an executive or judicial officer of any State, to support the Constitution of the United States, shall have engaged in insurrection or rebellion against the same, or given aid or comfort to the enemies thereof. But Congress may by a vote of two-thirds of each House, remove such disability.

Section 4. The validity of the public debt of the United States, authorized by law, including debts incurred for payment of pensions and bounties for service in suppressing insurrection or rebellion, shall not be questioned. But neither the United States nor any State shall assume or pay any debt or obligation incurred in aid of insurrection or rebellion against the United States, or any claim for the loss or emancipation of any slave; but all such debts, obligations and claims shall be held illegal and void.

Section 5. The Congress shall have power to enforce, by appropriate legislation, the provisions of this article.

July 9, 1868

Amendment 15
Black Suffrage Section 1. The right of citizens of the United States to vote shall not be denied or abridged by the United States or by any State on account of race, color, or previous condition of servitude.

Section 2. The Congress shall have power to enforce this article by appropriate legislation.

February 3, 1870.

Amendment 16
Income Taxes
The Congress shall have power to lay and collect taxes on incomes, from whatever source derived, without apportionment among the several States, and without regard to any census or enumeration.

February 3, 1913

Amendment 17

Senatorial Elections

The Senate of the United States shall be composed of two senators from each state, elected by the people thereof, for six years; and each Senator shall have one vote. The electors in each State shall have the qualifications requisite for electors of the most numerous branch of the State legislature.

When vacancies happen in the representation of any State in the Senate, the executive authority of such State shall issue writs of election to fill such vacancies: Provided, that the legislature of any State may empower the executive thereof to make temporary appointment until the people fill the vacancies by election as the legislature may direct.

This amendment shall not be so construed as to affect the election or term of any Senator chosen before it become valid as part of the Constitution.

April 8, 1913

Amendment 18

Prohibition of Liquor

Section 1. After one year from the ratification of this article, the manufacture, sale, or transportation of intoxicating liquors within, the importation thereof into, or the exportation thereof from the United States and all territory subject to the jurisdiction thereof for beverage purposes is hereby prohibited.

Section 2. The Congress and the several States shall have concurrent power to enforce this article by appropriate legislation.

Section 3. This article shall be inoperative unless it shall been ratified as an amendment to the Constitution by the legislatures of the several States, as provided in the Constitution, within seven tears from the date of the submission hereof to the States by the Congress.

January 16, 1919. Repealed by the Twenty-First Amendment, December 5, 1933.

Amendment 19
Women's Suffrage
The right of citizens of the United States to vote shall not be denied or abridged by the United States on account of sex.

Congress shall have power to enforce this article by appropriate legislation.

August 1920

Amendment 20
Terms Office
Section 1. The terms of the President and Vice-President shall end at noon the 20th day of January, and the terms of Senators and Representatives at noon on the 3rd day of January, of the years in which such terms would have ended if this article had not been ratified; and the terms of their successors shall then begin.

Section 2. The Congress shall assemble at least once in every year, and such meeting shall begin at noon on the 3rd day January, unless they shall by law appoint a different day.

Section 3. If, at the time fixed for the beginning of the term of the President, the President elect shall have died, the Vice-President elect shall become President. If a President shall not have been chosen before the time fixed for the beginning of his term, or if the President elect shall have failed to qualify, then the Vice-President elect shall act as President until a President shall manner in which one who is to act shall be selected, and such person shall act accordingly until a President or Vice-President shall have qualified.

Section 4. The Congress may by law provide for the case of the death of any of the persons from whom the house of Representative may choose a President whenever the right of choice shall have devolved upon them, and for the case of the death of any persons from whom the Senate may choose a Vice-President whenever the right of choice shall have devolved upon them.

Section 5. Section 1 and 2 shall take effect on the 15th day of October following the ratification of this article.

Section 6. This article shall be inoperative unless it shall have been ratified as an amendment to the Constitution by the legislature of three-fourths of the several States within seven years from the date of its submission.

January 23, 1933

Amendment 21
Repeal of Prohibition
Section 1. The eighteenth article of amendment to the Constitution of the United States is hereby repealed.

Section 2. The transportation or importation into and State, Territory, or possession of the United States for delivery or use therein of intoxicating liquors, in violation of the laws thereof, is hereby prohibited.

Section 3. The article shall be inoperative unless it shall have been ratified as an amendment to the Constitution by convention in the several States, as provided in the Constitution, within seven years from the date of the submission hereof to the States by the Congress.

December 5, 1933

Amendment 22
Terms Limits for the Presidency

Section 1. No person shall be elected to the office of the President more than twice, and on person who has held the office of President, or acted as President, for more than two years of a term to which some other person was elected to the office of the Article becomes operative from holing the office of President or acting as President during the remainder of such term.

Section 2. This article shall be inoperative unless it shall have been ratified as an amendment to the Constitution by the legislatures of three-fourths of the several States within seven years from the date of its submission to the States by the Congress.

February 27, 1951

Amendment 23
Washington, DC, Suffrage

Section 1. The district constituting the seat of government of the United States shall appoint in such manner as the Congress may direct:

A number of electors of President and Vice-President equal to the whole number of Senators and Representatives in Congress to which the District would be entitled if it were a state, but in no event more than the least populous State; they shall be in addition to those appointed by the States, but they shall be considered, for the purpose of the election of President and Vice-President, to be electors appointed by a State; and they shall meet in the District and perform such duties as provided by the twelfth article of amendment.

Section 2. The Congress shall have power to enforce this article by appropriate legislation.

Amendment 24
Abolition of Poll Taxes

Section 1. The right of citizens of the United States to vote in any primary or other election for President or Vice-President, for electors for President or Vice-President, or for Senator or Representative in Congress, shall not be denied or abridged by the United States or any State by reason of failure to pay any poll tax or other tax.

Section 2. The Congress shall have power to enforce this article by appropriate legislation.

January 23, 1964

Amendment 25
Presidential Succession

Section 1. In case of the removal of the President from office or of his death or resignation, Vice-President shall become President.

Section 2. Whenever there is a vacancy in the office of the Vice President, the President shall nominate a Vice-President who shall take office upon confirmation by a majority vote of both Houses of Congress.

Section 3. Whenever the President transmits to the President pro tempore of the Senate and the Speaker of the House of Representatives his written declaration that he is unable to discharge the powers of the duties of his office, and until he transmits to them a written declaration to the contrary, such powers and duties shall be discharged by the Vice-President as Acting President.

Section 4. Whenever the Vice-President and a majority of either the principal officers of the executive departments or of such other body as Congress may by law provide, transmit to the President pro tempore of the Senate and the Speaker of the House of Representatives their written declaration that the President is unable to discharge the powers and duties of his office, the

Vice-President shall immediately assume the powers and duties of the office as Acting President.

Thereafter, when the President transmits to the President pro tempore of the Senate and the Speaker of the House of Representatives his written declaration that no inability exists, he shall resume the powers and duties of his office unless the Vice-President and a majority of either the principal officers of the executive department or of such other body as Congress may by law provide, transmit within four days to the President pro tempore of the Senate and the House of Representatives their written declaration that the President is unable to discharge the powers and duties of his office. Thereupon Congress shall decide the issue, assembling within forty-hours for that purpose if not in session. If the Congress, within twenty-one days after receipt of the latter written declaration, or, if Congress is not in session, within twenty-one days after Congress is required to assemble, determines by two-thirds vote of both Houses that the President is unable to discharge the powers and duties of his office, the Vice-President shall continue to discharge the same as Acting President; otherwise; the President shall resume the powers and duties of his office.

February 10, 1967

Amendment 26
Eighteen-Year-Old Suffrage
Section 1. The right of citizens of the United States, who are eighteen years of age or older, to vote shall not be denied or abridged by the United States or by any State on account of age.

Section 2. The Congress shall have power to enforce this article by appropriate legislation.

June 30, 1971

Amendment 27
Congressional Pay Raises

No law, varying the compensation for the service of the Senators and Representatives, shall take effect, until an election of Representatives shall have intervened.

May 7, 1992. (Note: Congress submitted the text of this amendment as part of the proposed Bill of Rights on September 27, 1789. The Amendment was not ratified together with the first ten Amendments.)

MOTIVATION

Motivation is the positive attitude that is essential for achieving success in life. It is the inner drive that moves you to action. Even when you are discouraged or face setbacks, motivation can help you bounce back and keep on track. You may have skills, experience, intelligence, and talent, but you will accomplish little if you are not motivated to direct your energies toward specific goals *(Peak Performance, 54)*.

Both positive and negative needs and desires influence attitudes and motivation. The purpose of the "Train-Up a Child" nurturing mentoring model is to transform impossibilities into positively manifested realities. This is accomplished by teaching the at-risk the following principles:

- to learn to set goals and develop appropriate attitude/ behavior to achieve results
- to become masters at creating excellence by developing determination and perseverance
- to learn how to develop the inner strength to overcome incredible odds and surmount huge obstacles to learn how to become life leaders instead of life victims
- to develop high quality of living standards
- to learn how to employ creative thinking, problem solving, sound judgment, and effective decision making to manage everyday life and problems
- to learn how to develop healthy and nurturing relationships and communication
- to learn how to face fear with inner strength, confidence, and belief in oneself and the Lord Jesus Christ, who is God Almighty of the universe and all therein

To nurture/mentor one to wholeness, we must exercise our unbelievable power of loving simultaneously in the following ways:

- Empathize with at-risk people by listening from heart to heart.
- Show authentically your most deeply felt insights, learning, emotions, and convictions.
- Affirm the other person with a profound sense of belief, valuation, confirmation, appreciation, and encouragement.
- Pray with and for the at-risk people from the depth of your soul, tapping into the energy and wisdom of God the Holy Spirit.
- Sacrifice for the at-risk person, even going the second mile, doing far more than is expected, caring and serving until it sometimes hurts.

The primary laws of life (character traits) should be a deposit in people's emotional bank account. When you teach the primary laws of life, you are teaching empowering principles, and when they are understood, people will live by them. They trust the principles and trust themselves because they have integrity and their lives are integrated around a balanced set of principles that are universal, timeless, and self-evident. The at-risk people become conscious competence; they know what they are doing and why it works. It is taught both by precept and example; it enables people to effectively pass knowledge and skill from one generation to another by focusing on success principles: 1) building foundational skills; and 2) basic skills and strategies.

To build foundational skills, do the following:

- Focus on your strengths, not weaknesses; be a lifelong learner.
- Focus on character, not just skills; expand your emotional intelligence.
- Focus on priorities, not tasks; manage your time.
- Focus on planning, not reacting; maximizes your resources.

To develop basic skills and strategies, focus on the following:

- the message, not the presentation—listen and take effective notes
- the meaning, not the words—active reading
- the sum, not the parts—improve your memory skills
- understanding, not testing-excel at test taking
- application and excellence, not perfection—express yourself in writing and speech
- critical thinking, not assumptions—become a critical thinker and a creative problem solver
- cooperation, not judgment—build supportive and diverse relationships
- success, not failure—develop positive habits
- accomplishments, not entitlement-explore majors and careers

THE SEVEN EAGLE
CHARACTERISTICS

For the African-American church to be highly effective in the at-risk endeavor, it must activate principles. They must also develop in and possess the seven leadership characteristics of the eagle.

1. The eagle is *fearless*: It will attack its prey no matter the size, even a mountain goats and snakes. Leaders have to defend their future.

2. The eagle is *tenacious (courageous and strong):* It is persistent in seeking things that are valued or desired. An eagle looks for and flies into storms. A leader uses storms (challengers) and doesn't run from them. To leaders, storms are tools used for development. Leaders do not wish things were easier but that things were better.

3. The eagle is *nurturing:* The eagle is known for its ferociousness. However, it is gentle and attentive to its young, and at just the right time the mother eagle teaches her eaglets how to fly. If the eaglet is cowardly, she returns to the nest, tears it apart, and nudges the eaglet off the cliff. Her message to the eaglet is, *"Fly or die."*

4. The eagle is *a high flier:* Eagles can fly up to an altitude of ten thousand feet, but they are able to swiftly dive up to fifty to sixty miles an hour and land on the ground. Leaders are down to earth. You may be the top dog in your position, but you must be able to touch people. You have to know how to fly back down to earth swiftly. You must be relatable. The family members must know you, like you,

and trust you. That is not possible at ten thousand feet in the air.

5. The eagle *never eats dead meat*: It hunts for and kills its own food. It hunts for the prey while it is warm and alive. Leaders must go where the action is. Leaders hunt down and find lively people to grow their businesses.

6. The eagle is full of *vitality*: The eagle is full of life and it has the power to endure. By the time the eagle reaches about thirty years old, life gets hard. Its physical condition has deteriorated to the point where survival is difficult. Its talons (claws) lose flexibility and cannot properly grip its prey. Its beak becomes dull and bent; its wing feathers get heavy and dull, which impairs flight ability. Now, does the eagle cry, "Woe *is me!*" and curl up in a ball and die? No! The eagle retreats to a mountaintop, and over a five-month period, it goes through a metamorphosis.

- It knocks off its own beak by banging it against a rock.
- It plucks out its talons.
- It plucks out its feathers.

Each stage produces a re-growth of the removed body parts. After metamorphosis, the eagle lives another thirty to forty years. As leaders, we have to renew ourselves through personal development and constant learning. Leaders must have a holistic approach to life: spiritually, physically, intellectually, community, and emotionally (SPICE).

7. The eagle has *keen (sharp) vision*: The eagle's eyes are specially designed for long-distance focus and clarity. Eagles can spot another eagle soaring from fifty miles away. Eagles have strong vision and are able to identify their prey and focus on it until they gets the prey, and at the same time they are able to see from afar their enemies, like the snakes trying to sneak into their nests to steal their eggs

or kill their young ones. Though eagles build their nests on high rocks and places, snakes have the tendency and ability to climb it. But the strong vision of the eagle keeps the enemies away from its nest. All leaders must have vision that is big and focused. A big, focused vision will always produce big results.

And Step, Inc.'s big, focused vision is that within twenty years, 80 percent of the pariahs will go through the "Train-Up a Child" nurturing/mentoring model:

- Every African-American child will be ready for any university at high school graduation.
- The family caregivers will have access to careers with salary and a complete financial package, including both family healthcare and retirement benefits.
- They live in safe, decent, and affordable housing on fair terms.
- The pariah community will become equitable, sustainable, and desirable.

With Christ the omnipresent, omnipotent, and omniscience in our souls, there is nothing or no one to stop the plan of God.

IN CLOSING

"If you cannot run with the big dogs, stay on the porch." And Step, Inc. is not only running with the big dogs, but it is also leading the pack.

The story goes this way. There were three dogs that came across a bone—two big dogs and one little dog (a puppy). The two big dogs began fighting over the bone. While they were fighting, the little dog walked over to the bone, and with his mouth, he picked the bone up and went into hiding and began eating it; there was a lot of meat on the bone. When the two big dogs finished fighting, they looked and the little dog and the bone were gone.

And Step, Inc. is the little dog that has discovered there is a lot of healthy meat on this bone. Locked up in these children and youth is the key to innovative economy, entrepreneurs in regenerative medicine: doctors, biologists, chemists, physicists, bioengineers, and biotechnologists, just to name a few. How can segregationists or the African-American elitists reject the one who may hold the key to their life expansion or progeny? Treachery creates spiritual blindness.

After Jesus' resurrection, Peter and six disciples went fishing. Jesus appeared to them along the shore of Lake Tiberias (John 21). Jesus asked Peter three times, "Do you love Me?" Jesus' three demands were the following:

1. Feed My lambs. (Nurture the spiritual babies.)
2. Take care of My sheep. (Minister to all adults.)
3. Feed My sheep. (Teach them Bible doctrine.)

We *are not authorized to quit until the church is raptured.*

BIBLIOGRAPHY

Alexander, Michelle. *The New Jim Crow: Mass Incarceration in the Age of Colorblindness.* New York: New York Press, 2010.

The Holy Bible: Contemporary English Vision. New York: American Bible Society, 1995.

Benner, David, G., Editor. *Baker Encyclopedia of Psychology*: Grand Rapids, MI: Baker Book House, 1999.

Boy Scouts of America. *American Labor:* Merit Badge Series. Irving, TX: Boy Scouts of America, 2008.

Cannon, Katie G. *Black Womanist Ethics.* Atlanta, GA: Scholars Press, 1988.

Cosby, Bill & Poussaint, Alvin F. *Come On, People: On the Path from Victims to Victors.* Nashville, TN: Thomas Nelson, 2007.

Covey, Sean. *The 7 Habits of Highly Effective Teens: A true gift for the teenage soul.* New York: Fireside, 1998.

Covey, Stephen R. *The 7 Habits of Highly Effective Families:* New York: Golden Books, 1997.

____ *Principle-Centered Leadership:* New York: Free Press, 2003. ---- *The Eighth Habit: From Effectiveness to Greatness.* New York: Free Press, 2004.

Downes, John, A.B. *Dictionary of Finance & Investment Terms.* Hauppauge, NY: Barron's Educational Series, Inc., 2006.

Eagleston, Lotya Ann. "Social Ministry." *Beaver County Times.* April 19, 1993. Section C-1

Ferret, Sharon K. *Peak Performance: Success in College and Beyond.* New York: McGraw-Hill, 2010.

Foster, Charles R., and Grant S. Shockley, eds. *Working with Black Youth: Opportunities for Christian Ministry.* Nashville, TN: Abingdon Press, 1989.

Harrington, Judith B. *The Everything Start Your Own Business Book, 2nd edition*. Avon, MA: F+W Publication, Inc., 2006.

Kunjufu, Jawanza. *Keeping Black Boys out of Special Education*. Chicago, IL: African American, 2005.

June, Lee N., editor. *The Black Family: Past, Present, Future*. Grand Rapids, MI: Zondervan Publishing House, 1991.

Kaplan Financial. *Series 6 License Exam Manual 3rd Edition: Investment Company Products/Variable Contracts Limited Representative Exam*. United States of America: DF Institute, Inc. 2007.

Kimbro, Dennis; and Hill, Napoleon. *Think and Grow Rich: A Black Choice*. New York: Fawcett Columbine, 1991.

Kunjufu, Jawanza. *Adam! Where Are You? Why Most Black Men Don't Go to Church*. Chicago, IL: African American Images, 1994.

Kunjufu, Jawanza. *Hip-Hop vs. MAAT: A Psycho/Social Analysis of Values*. Chicago, IL: African American Images, 1993.

Miller, Craig Kennet. *Baby Boomer Spirituality: Ten Essential Values of a Generation*. Nashville, TN: Discipleship Resources, 1993.

Oshinsky, David M. *Worse than Slavery: Parchman Farm and the Ordeal of Jim Crow Justice*. CITY, STATE New York: Free Press Paperbacks, 1996

Schaller, Lyle E. ed. *Center City Churches: The New Urban Frontier*. Nashville, TN: Abingdon Press, 1993.

Staley, Sheila R. *The Black Family: Past, Present, & Future*. Grand Rapids, MI: Zondervan Publishing House, 1991.

Thieme, R.B., Jr. *Christian Integrity*. Houston, TX: R.B. Thieme, Jr. Bible Ministries, 2002.

____ *Christian Suffering*. Houston, TX: R.B. Thieme, Jr. Bible Ministries, 2002.

Divine Guidance. Houston, TX: R.B. Thieme, Jr. Bible Ministries, 1999.

____. *Freedom through Military Victory*. Houston, TX: R.B. Thieme, Jr. Bible Ministries, 2003.

____. *Heathenism*. Houston, TX: R.B. Thieme, Jr. Bible Ministries, 2001.

____*King of Kings and Lord of Lords*. Houston, TX: R.B. Thieme, Jr. Bible Ministries, 2004

____. *Mental Attitude Dynamics.* Houston, TX: R.B. Thieme, Jr. Bible Ministries, 2000.

____. *Old Sin Nature vs. Holy Spirit.* Houston, TX: R.B. Thieme, Jr. Bible Ministries, 2000.

____. *Reversionism.* Houston, TX: R.B. Thieme, Jr. Bible Ministries, 2000.

____. *Slave Market of Sin.* Houston, TX: R.B. Thieme, Jr. Bible Ministries, 1994.

____. *Satan and Demonism.* Houston, TX: R.B. Thieme, Jr. Bible Ministries, 1996.

____. *The Angelic Conflict.* Houston, TX: R.B. Thieme, Jr. Bible Ministries, 2012.

____. *The Divine Outline of History: Dispensations and the Church.* Houston, TX: R.B. Thieme, Jr. Bible Ministries, 1999.

____. *The Integrity of God.* Houston, TX: R.B. Thieme, Jr. Bible Ministries, 2005.

____. *The Plan of God.* Houston, TX: R.B. Thieme, Jr. Bible Ministries, 2003.

____. *The Trinity.* Houston, TX. R.B. Thieme, Bible Ministries, 2003.

____· *Tongues.* Houston, TX: R.B. Thieme, Jr. Bible Ministries, 2000.

Train Up a Child. Houston, TX: R.B. Thieme, Jr. Bible Ministries, 2008.

____. *Witnessing.* Houston, TX: R.B. Thieme, Jr. Bible Ministries, 1992.

Wiegand, Steve. *U.S. History for Dummies: Making Everything Easier.* Hoboken, NY: Wiley Publishing, 2009.

Weisbord, Marvin & Janoff, Sandra. *Future Search: An Action Guide to Finding Common Ground in Organizations on Communities.* San Francisco, CA: Berrett-Koehler, 2000.

CPSIA information can be obtained
at www.ICGtesting.com
Printed in the USA
BVHW012341200921
617161BV00002B/48